M

Nigel Dempster's Royal Diary

Has Charles found his future bride?

Wives who guide his

THE two happily married women who influence Prince Charles most on personal matters, Lady Tryon and Camilla Parker Bowles, have both given the heir to the throne their approval over his new choice of girlfriend.

Now the way is clear for Charles, 32 on November 14, to plight his troth to Lady Diana Spencer, who, friends tell me, has secretly worshipped him for most of her life—her father, Earl Spencer, was equerry to the Queen on her accession.

A few months ago close friends of Charles met to discuss his dilemma—whenever he became keen on a nubile young lady with a history, her previous love life would be paraded through the Press. And no future Queen of England can afford a past.

In fact, Prince Charles and Anna Wallace blame me for ending their romance when I disclosed on May 28 that she had spent three years with two former lovers, banker Alan Morris, 47, and stockbroker David Coaten, 38.

SCOTS landowner's daughter Anna Wallace can thank her dismissal from the royal scene in part to Australian Dale Tryon, wife of banker Lord Tryon whose father was the Queen's Treasurer, and to Camilla Parker Bowles, 33.

Quite simply, they did not take to her and told Charles, with whom they enjoy a close and confidential friendship, as much. My report about her former loves only served to back up their opinion and Anna's days were numbered. Niece of Lord Ashcombe, head of the Cubitt building family, Camilla married Roman Catholic Andrew Parker Bowles—a former boyfriend of Princess Anne—in 1973. He is a colonel, aged 40, in the Household Cavalry. Both attractive ladies have children and Charles is godfather to Charles Tryon, four, and Thomas Parker Bowles, nearly six. Not by coincidence is Charles's new country estate near the Gloucestershire home of Andrew and Camilla.

Dale, 32, who says that Charles refers to her affectionately as 'Kanga,' has been his hostess on many occasions at the 700-acre Tryon country estate near Salisbury and, with her husband, was salmon fishing last month in Iceland with Charles as usual.

When he made an official visit to Australia, Dale flew home to Melbourne—her father,

*Colonel a
Charl*

Barry Harp
on hand to
to introduce
None of thi
with Charle
bow or curt
It is only in
any familia

good time to marry, spen
early part of this year
Anna, 25, but after a ro
meat millionaire Lord Ve
country home, she met, Jo

NIGEL DEMPSTER

and the death of discretion

NIGEL DEMPSTER

and the death of discretion

TIM WILLIS

First published in 2010 by

Short Books
3A Exmouth House
Pine Street
EC1R 0JH

10 9 8 7 6 5 4 3 2 1

ISBN 978-1-906021- 84-9

Printed in Great Britain by Clays, Suffolk

Cover design: Emily Fox
Image copyright for colour plate section:
13, 19, 20, 22 © Alan Davidson.
8, 12, 16, 17, 18, 23, 24, 25 © Press Association
4, 5, 6, 7, 9, 10, 11, 15, 21, 26, 27 © Getty Images
Front cover image © Getty Images
Back cover image © *Daily Mail*

For Queenie

CONTENTS

INTRODUCTION   13

1   RISE
The Making of a Deb's Delight   23

2   SHINE
The Socially Mobile Sixties   53

3   POWER
'The Biggest Gossip in the World'   81

4   GLORY
The Toast of the Turf   107

5   POMP
The Former Greatest Living Englishman   141

6   CIRCUMSTANCE
'Now People Expose Themselves'   165

7   DECLINE
A Surfeit of Diaries   193

8   FALL
'I Feel Very Discombobulated'   217

INDEX   242

'If the trade of the gossip columnist is trivial,
then all life is trivial'
— Nigel Dempster

'To a philosopher all news is gossip'
— Henry David Thoreau

INTRODUCTION

Future generations may wonder how, in less than 50 years, Britain's generally tame press transformed itself into a celebrity circus where reality TV stars held the front pages with the details of their sex lives. What caused such changes in the media, its audience and subjects? To some extent, the answer is Nigel Dempster (1941-2007).

The life and works of the late gossip columnist inform and entertain at so many levels. His wine-soaked journey through old Fleet Street and Society is a tragi-comic romp. His chronicles of the upper classes afford a wealth of opportunities to devour and condemn the follies of an extinct species. And when these themes are set against a history of the media over Dempster's lifetime, we can see how and why society with a small 's' has been so transformed – and how and why he flourished. As he would say when on his high horse, social trends are as important to history as economic and political ones. The devil is in the detail.

For a quarter of the 20th century, Dempster was the man perfectly placed and qualified to record – and accelerate – the end of the age of deference, the transfer of wealth from the aristocrats to plutocrats, and the collapse of standards in the old Establishment. The highest paid journalist in Britain, as much a brand as a person, he was a vital resource at the *Daily Mail*. It is, then, an irony that the genre to which he contributed so much eventually left him behind. However, the sphere in which he succeeded was created in the shadow of the *Sun*, and one day his brand of journalism would be eclipsed.

In the Nineties, he often used to say as much to me: 'The stories that should be in my column are now front-page news.' And it's true that, to profit and survive, the British press had become less about public interest than the public's interest. But Dempster's value had also declined. Long before his enforced retirement, supermodels and footballers were shoving aside his roster of ragged gentry and ageing jet-setters; and the competition from gossip magazines was ever fiercer. Then again, it may be that he was simply a by-product and a casualty of broadcasting.

I defy anyone to make an absolute distinction between gossip and news – or the means of gathering them. But it is clear that, as the public began to take its information from the airwaves, the printed press became more a medium of entertainment, in a process that is still continuing. Like some ageing leading lady, Dempster may simply have served his purpose.

I first encountered him in 1986, when I rang for a quote to insert into a piece that I was writing. The next year, when I was in the *Mail* offices off Fleet Street, I saw him across the desks, striding to his corner room, while shouting, 'I own this place, I own this place! If it wasn't for me you'd all be in the gutter' and in 1990, we became better acquainted at the *Sunday Times*, where I ghost-wrote a feature for him. (Dempster had somehow wangled a commission to puff one of his books – with no seeming intention of fulfilling it.)

Though I can't say we were close, we got on well enough for him to come for supper at home, where he regaled us with ungallant tales about a former conquest who was also great friends with another guest. ('She was a fluffy little thing – fine down all over her.') He was the last to leave and when I was briefly out of the room, he came on pretty strong to my then-wife. Luckily, she was more amused than shocked – and so, I'm afraid, was I – for Dempster was one of those characters who could get away with almost anything because they made you laugh. I seem to recall he pinched my bottom on the way out.

He was a camp figure, with a signet ring on his pinky, wearing too-tight suits from which as the *Evening Standard*'s editor Geordie Greig puts it, 'his arse protruded like an apple'. But at the top of his game, such was his power and influence that two kings – Hussein of Jordan and Constantine of Greece – were once seen queuing up to greet him in Harry's Bar. At the *Mail*, it is remembered that when the last proprietor needed distraction or his wife attention, Dempster would be wheeled out to entertain them. 'He was family,' they say. 'Vere [the 3rd Viscount Rothermere] and Bubbles loved him.' But so did the less exalted. 'Good on yer, Nigel,' the travellers at the Epsom Derby would shout when he arrived in Lord White's helicopter. He was renowned for the lavish Christmas boxes he gave to the lads who liveried his horses.

My Purple Prose, Chatty Corner and Superfluous, Aardwolf, Switch and Pretoria Dancer, Rhyming Prose and General Gossip; over the years, Dempster's readers would get to know all these beasts through his columns – and many characters from the track. Investing huge amounts of time and money in racing and gambling, he was a different man – if as much himself – in this other life, and I can only apologise to the turf fraternity if my allotted sum of words is not adequate to do it justice.

I must apologise, too, to some of the victims of Dempster's vicious temper. Most of those on the receiving end – particularly his staff – came to see it as the flipside of his generosity, but a minority may feel that, while I have touched on a couple of notorious incidents, they hardly give a taste of his tyranny. I hope the aggrieved will understand that I have given some regard to his medical condition.

True, he had a foul mouth and was quite capable of manhandling his assistants, long before he had any excuse except a sore head from drink. In his later career, he spent hours every day firing off memos to people sitting only feet away from him. He once threatened a female member of his staff with dismissal for conceiving, and sent her a note saying 'How dare you get pregnant?'. But the horrible illness that led to his death at 65 – progressive supranuclear palsy – can incubate for up to fifteen years, manifesting itself slowly at first, before suddenly accelerating. Its symptoms include paranoid delusions and violent mood swings. Although it was only diagnosed three or four years before his death, it may have been with him for half his working life.

Another thing. To some, the rehearsal of Dempster's greatest stories will seem old news. I can only reply that to most readers – even other journalists – they are now ancient history, and need to be re-told. I am more troubled that I could only include a fraction of the tens of thousands of items that appeared under Dempster's name. Nor could I mention or interview every significant friend, colleague, contact and enemy. They were myriad, as one would expect of the world's greatest gossip columnist – and from most he earned some kind of respect. Take the playwright Tom Stoppard, who can't have relished having his love life plastered all over the papers. When I mentioned to him that I was writing this book, he was surprisingly generous. 'Dempster wrote some pretty unpleasant things,' said Stoppard. 'But unlike most of his kind, he was generally accurate. And when one met him, at least he told the truth.'

Still, I come not to praise Dempster; he was virtuous

neither in public nor private. He did a job that you may condone or condemn according to your lights. But he was a phenomenon, of a type now disappeared. And through his eyes we can view the world – long swept away – that he broached, moved in and reported on. Here, titles commanded respect, and white tie was worn at balls where bands played dance tunes to which teenage couples knew the steps. The indiscretions of the Royal Family could not be noised abroad without damaging national stability. Drinking and driving was more a challenge than a crime. And the lower orders were kept behind the green baize door – until Dempster threw it open.

Of course, he didn't achieve this single-handedly. A gossip columnist is only as good as his sources, his colleagues, his staff and their informants. And while some scandalous stories that appear in the press may be literally overheard at dinner and parties, more often they have been paid for. There are few true secrets in this world, and we rely on our friends and associates to keep ours. But if they can profit from divulging them, and escape being traced, only the best are less greedy than scrupulous.

Adam Helliker, Dempster's deputy for 16 years, paints this scenario: 'Let's say you go to a private view, and there are some "social" people there. You introduce yourself as a diarist to one of them, start chatting and they tell you something innocuous but interesting. You say: "Can I use that in the column?" and because it's harmless, they agree. So on publication, you send them a cheque – and before long, they will be ringing you with tidbits. It's hard for them to resist when they can earn a couple of hundred for a five-minute phone call.'

In this account, perhaps I should devote more space to the stories that Dempster got wrong (and God knows, we all have done) but I hope the examples given are sufficiently striking to remind readers that he was far from infallible. Besides, it has been difficult enough to separate truth from fiction in his life without subjecting his output to the same scrutiny. Often, as in the New Testament, there are several versions of the same story. Moreover, memories fade or become embroidered, confidences are sometimes kept and – call it exaggeration, anecdotage or plain lying – when it suits them, many of Dempster's circle can have as tenuous a hold on the truth as he could at times. You can't always tell if they speak in earnest or sport, out of mischief or malice. You wonder if *they* can. From them, however, I exclude nearly all the following, to whom I am indebted for their time and help: Lady Elizabeth Anson, Robert Barrett, Drusilla Beyfuss, Liz Brewer, Charlie Brooks, Tina Brown, Carolyne Christie, Michael Cole, Charles Collingwood, Michael Corry-Reid, Jeremy Cox, Emma de Bendern, Atalanta de Bendern, Tessa Dahl, Louisa Dempster, Pam Dempster, Michael Dupree, Anne Esplen, Robin Esser, Peter Evans, Rod Gilchrist, Geordie Greig, Anthony Haden-Guest, Nicholas Haslam, Adam Helliker, Audrey Hoare, Richard Ingrams, Richard Kay, Nicky Kerman, Mary Killen, Ulla Kloster, Geoffrey Levy, Sir Roderic Llewellyn, Colin Mackenzie, John McEntee, Peter McKay, Robert Mills, Lady Camilla

Osborne, Michael Proudlock, David Radcliffe, Christopher Rhys-Jones, Glenys Roberts, Lady Jacqueline Rufus-Isaacs, Lord Antony Rufus-Isaacs, Erika Sciama, Ingrid Seward, Nick Simunek, Felicity Swan, Taki Theodoracopulos, Diana Tremlett, Ed Victor, Christopher Wilson, Anna Wintour and the Duchess of York. I must also thank Paul Dacre, for sanctioning my approaches to journalists from the *Daily Mail,* and for allowing me access to the Associated Newspapers library, whose staff – not least Jonathan Bain and Mo McFarland – were of unfailing assistance.

July 2010

RISE
The Making of a Deb's Delight

It was often claimed – not least by Nigel Dempster himself – that being Australian gave him license to comment so freely on the foibles of Britain's rich, famous and titled. 'In this job,' he once said, 'you have to be a foreigner.' But that wasn't strictly true: although his father was Australian, Dempster's mother was English, and he always held a British passport. Again, his colonial background was cited as proof of his outsider status. But while he was born and initially raised in India, Dempster spent little time in the continent after the age of six, and enjoyed an extremely privileged life when he was there. No, what really set him apart from most of his British peers was his family antecedents – and the distinctly odd marriage contracted by his parents, Eric and Angela.

Eric Richard Pratt Dempster – later known as 'Demy' – was from one of the distinguished and wealthy pioneer families, originally from Scotland. Born in Beverley, Western Australia, in 1893, he was the middle of three sons of James Pratt Dempster and Charlotte Patton – and also a half-brother to Jock Dempster (the child of Charlotte's sister Louisa, whom James had first married, and who died soon after). James was unusually old to have young children, having married Louisa Patton at the age of 50 and Charlotte at 55. Burdened by the death of his first wife, and unhappy with his second, he took to drink, and after falling down some cellar steps, died at the age of 73. His widow left the family property to be sorted out by her stepson Jock, and sailed back to Britain with her children.

Demy qualified in Mining Engineering at the Camborne School in Cornwall – and when it turned out that Jock and the lawyers had made off with his mother's inheritance, it was he who would support her. His first job, in India, was at the Kolar Gold Fields, near Bangalore. Also working there, as an analyst, was Jack Stephens, originally from Devon and a decade his senior. They became friends, and when Jack's only child Angela was just ten years old, Demy declared that he was going to marry her when she grew up. This he duly did, as soon as her parents would allow the wedding, which took place two days after her eighteenth birthday.

Angela 'Topsy' Stephens was born in Britain in 1909, taken to India soon after, and spent her next 47 years there.

She was possessed of neither brains nor beauty, but Demy was madly in love with her, as evidenced by his letters to her in the months before their wedding. Writing in September 1926 from London, where he was on bi-annual leave, he called her his 'sweet little wife-to-be' and his 'darlingest'. 'We marry in January, so we may have to be firm about it,' he declared, and added: 'I revere, idolise and worship you. No one could be more loved than I love you, my preciousest.'

He adored the elfin-faced Topsy for the rest of his days, and being 16 years her senior, always regarded her as his child bride. He was a handsome man, possibly the most eligible in Kolar, and she no doubt gloated over capturing him at such a young age. According to Nigel's elder sister Erika, Topsy looked on Demy as her 'rock', and retained her girlishness with him throughout their 55-year marriage.

In its own strange way, says Erika, 'their relationship worked well – although ostensibly they had very little in common'. An almost militant atheist, Demy was essentially a serious man with a good brain, who preferred a quiet life. He swam and played golf and tennis most days. He appreciated a game of bridge, and in retirement was addicted to the *Daily Telegraph* crossword and newspaper, along with the *Financial Times*. Above all, he loved his work.

Topsy played tennis but not golf and only swam to combat the heat, with her head held high. She enjoyed riding and walking, and went out in the cool of the evening while Demy was on the golf course. She was very good at the Chinese game of *mahjong* – much favoured by the *memsahibs* – but perhaps most enjoyed playing the piano, which she had studied at school. Only vaguely religious, she very likely lived without a serious thought in her head, under the protection of her older husband on whom she depended utterly. She loved life even when she was very old, and it was probably her gaiety that attracted people. She had a happy, optimistic nature and was very sociable. However, even Erika describes her as 'a rather shallow person', as snobbish and bigoted as so many of her contemporaries.

The couple had three children to whom Topsy was a fond and easy-going mother: the eldest, Pam, in 1930, Erika in 1938 and Nigel in 1941. Demy was a proud father, though somewhat uninvolved – and enraged by bad behaviour. So, says Pam, while Topsy thought her son 'a gift from the gods, who she thoroughly ruined', he became Demy's *bête noire*, and there were regular battles. Topsy would always take the side of this naughty, defiant and ungovernable boy, which made Demy jealous of him. But that seems a strange reaction, when one considers how phlegmatically he accepted his wife's more serious failings.

Perhaps Topsy's morals inspired her son's lifelong interest in extra-marital adventures. For despite her husband's unalloyed affection, she still found other men irresistible. Her infidelities started soon after they were married and took place right under his nose. On their honeymoon, Demy found her with another man in their cabin. But, he turned a blind eye – and it wasn't until he was in his late eighties, and starting to decline mentally, that he took it into his head to try and close his wife's bank account, because she was seeing somebody else.

He had quite a list to choose from; among them a mines-company doctor, a Canadian Royal Air Force pilot stationed at Dum-Dum during the war and – most curiously, considering Topsy's prejudices – the striking West Indian crooner, Leslie 'Hutch' Hutchinson. Remembered for the white handkerchief that he would pull from his top pocket to mop his brow, Hutch was one of the first cabaret singers to tour big theatres, and was world-famous before the conflict.

One can understand her fascination. Born in 1900, satirised in Evelyn Waugh's *Decline and Fall* and a one-time friend of Edward Prince of Wales, the bisexual Hutch numbered among his previous conquests Tallulah Bankhead, Merle Oberon, Cole Porter and Ivor Novello. Possibly, in the early Fifties, he had dalliances with Princess Margaret and her aunt Princess Marina; and most scandalously, during the Thirties, he regularly serviced Edwina Mountbatten, who is said to have bought the impressively endowed Grenadan a diamond-encrusted penis sheath. (It is also alleged that the pair once had to be separated by doctors, after the Countess suffered an attack of the muscle-tightening condition vaginismus.)

Although Hutch's affair with the future Vicereine of India was never public knowledge in her lifetime, Buckingham Palace and such press barons as Lord Beaverbrook were aware of it, and conspired to ruin his career. So by the time Topsy met him – in 1955 at Quaglino's, on one of the Dempsters' bi-annual visits to London – he was in decline, overweight and drinking heavily. 'She asked him to her table after the floorshow,' says Erika, whom her mother had taken that evening, 'and it turned out that he was going to play in Calcutta. So when we got back, she brought me along again, as cover, as well as a friend of mine.' While the young ones went around town, Topsy and Hutch got to know each other better.

Around this time, Erika believes that Demy became impotent after a prostate operation. Whatever the reason, Topsy's romance was resumed when she and her husband moved to Britain two years later, and lasted in one form or another until Hutch died in 1969, broke and long out of fashion. Although he knew about it from his teens – when Topsy introduced him to her exotic lover – Nigel Dempster never chose to publicise this particular affair. While insinuating himself into smart parties in the late Fifties, he probably thought it best not to mention that his mother was dating the sad black singer on the stage.

***

By the end of World War II, the Dempster family was all in India together, unable to travel abroad – and by then Demy's work had taken him from Kolar up to Bihar. Here he started as Mines Superintendent at the Indian Copper Corporation (the second largest copper mines in the world) and some years later rose to the top position of General Manager. At first, he lived in a European enclave near the mines at Mosaboni. But on his promotion, he crossed the great Subarnarekha River and was allocated the best company bungalow at Moubhandar, where the smelting and administration took place. From nearby, one could take the railway to the town of Jamshedpur, 40 miles away, or – for any real shopping or entertainment – to Calcutta, which was a further 160 miles.

Nigel was born at Miss Riordan's Nursing Home in Calcutta on 1 November 1941, and enjoyed a happy childhood, without schooling or much restraint. At Moubhandar, he lived in some luxury. Two sleepy Ghurkas in sentry boxes guarded the entrance to the General Manager's house, and the family bungalow was set in verdant gardens, which also contained a goldfish pond in its own brick building and a separate vegetable garden, where carrots jostled for space with mangos. The smaller of the two sitting rooms was even air-conditioned, and the family would gather here to listen to the World Service and gramophone records from the old country, among them the works of Topsy's future paramour, Hutch.

It was a large household, employing a dozen *malis* (gardeners), two bearers who managed the house and waited at table, an *ayah* to look after the children, several *jemidars* (sweepers and cleaners), a *sice* (groom), a driver called Anthony, and a *dhobi wallah* who dealt with the laundry, which was done in the river. The cook and his helpers prepared food in the European style, except on Sundays, when *tiffin* (a curry lunch) was served. Bathed and changed, the whole family always met for tea at five o' clock.

The Dempsters kept a pony, a goat for milk, chickens, four ducks – Eenie, Meenie, Minee and Mo, who were originally intended for the table but became pets – and a pair of green parrots called Peter and Paul, who lived free in the garden but would come and sit on the dining table at meal times. There were always dogs – generally terriers, which were ceremoniously buried after death in miniature concrete tombs with inscriptions – and cats, whose lives were usually shortened by the jackals that emerged from the jungle at night.

Next to the residence was the company golf course, where Demy played after work; over the river was the company club, scene of a weekly film screening and various social functions; and a short walk away was the company swimming pool, where the children spent much of their time. While Pam was sent away to school, the other two received a minimal education from Topsy – with limited success in Nigel's case. 'Any attempt on her part to teach him was met with fury,' says Pam. 'He would hurl the books across the verandah and into the garden.'

The *ayah* couldn't deal with him at all and sometimes he required male persuasion – Anthony the driver being summoned to dress him after his bath. Erika remembers Nigel throwing his breakfast eggs at an unfortunate bearer. Pam recalls him drinking the water from the dogs' bowls. Still, as *chota sahib* the son and heir was regarded with exaggerated respect by the servants and no effort was spared to please him. A muscular child, he learned to walk when he was only nine months old, and by the age of two he was driving off the verandah with a set of miniature golf clubs commissioned by his father. He once used an iron to beat Erika about the head, and was impervious to the chastisements of his father. Demy must have had mixed feelings in 1947, when he and Topsy took their beloved son to Britain by liner.

Their destination was South Devon, where Jack Stephens and his wife had retired in the late Thirties (eventually to be joined by Demy's mother, who took a house in nearby Littleham). The two girls had preceded Nigel, and for some remuneration, had been lodging with Angela's aged parents when they were not at boarding school. On the expiration of his leave, Demy returned to India while Topsy stayed behind a few months, to settle in her son at her parents' house. Nigel was first sent to a primary school called Woodlands – whose alumni were known as 'Woodlice' – and then to St Peter's, a tiny pre-prep school in Exmouth run by Theophilus Rhys-Jones, the grandfather of Sophie, who is currently married to Prince Edward. There, Sophie's father Christopher – who was briefly one of Nigel's teachers – remembers him as 'a personable young man' who, when his daughter joined the Royal Family, 'always played with a straight bat – what he printed was accurate, unlike the ridiculous things in many of the other papers'.

According to Pam, Angela Dempster wrote to her son every week, but at his outset as a boarder, Nigel just stuffed the letters into his tuck box. When the matron discovered this, she made enquiries – and it transpired that he couldn't read them. This may have been a reflection on his mother's hand, but points to a certain lack of intellectual curiosity – or filial affection. However, Nigel was active in other areas, playing in the first eleven at both cricket and soccer, 'and generally being in the thick of everything,' remembers his old classmate David Radcliffe.

'He always knew everyone's business and what was going on before the rest of us. He was always at the front of the queue when it mattered, always the first with a new craze. I'd say he was more streetwise than the rest of us – and more charming, more energetic. You might say he was pushy. The rest of us local boys either belonged to the Budleigh Salterton tennis club set, or the one at Exmouth [the Cranford Club], but he managed to be part of both.'

Nigel remembered school coach trips across Dartmoor as a high point of his Devon days: 'We would press our noses to the windows to catch sight of the chain gangs of prisoners… and one or two would humorously make the motion of thumbing for a lift.' In general, though, life was far from exciting. On Saturdays, Nigel and Erika went to the cinema in Exeter, on Sundays to church with Granny.

Throughout his school days, if he was to escape such torpor, Nigel needed to cultivate boys who could invite him to their family homes – and luckily, he showed a flair for friendship (keeping up with some St Peter's pupils for the rest of his life). He also showed a flair for mischief. Although some of Jack's charm rubbed off on him, the osteoporotic Granny Stephens found him hard to handle. After a series of incidents involving his catapult and neighbours' windows, he was sent to live for a few weeks with a Miss Sweet in Exmouth.

'I learned at an early age to fend for myself,' Nigel once said. 'I wasn't homesick because we didn't have a home.' He only saw his parents in the summer – alternately visiting and being visited from India – but enjoyed some expensive holidays when he did. In 1950, he and his sisters were taken on a three-week motoring holiday through France, Switzerland and Italy, spending twelve days at Menton. After a grand tour of the Pommery & Greno champagne cellars, the family was ushered into the manager's office to share a bottle (enjoyed not least by Nigel, who afterwards insisted on lying down on the back seat of the car with his legs dangling out of the window). In 1952, they were off again, this time for six and a half weeks and on a different route through France, Switzerland and Italy, also taking in the Austrian Tyrol. But if Nigel derived any cultural benefit from these juvenile bouts of travels, he did not evince it when sitting his Common Entrance exams for Sherborne, the ancient college in Dorset. On the first attempt he failed. However, Mr Rhys-Jones persuaded the school to let him re-sit at St Peter's the following term and – with the help of some unorthodox invigilating – he miraculously passed.

***

In middle age, Nigel Dempster would have mixed feelings about Sherborne, which he joined in January 1955. On the one hand, he became a regular at old boys' functions, and heaped compliments on the school in his column. On the other, he would tell his second wife that he 'hated' the place – 'that Sunday night feeling, when you had to be back in bounds' – and that it had stunted his emotions. Whichever, it cramped his style. The acquisition of a drop-handled racing bike had allowed him to embark on a social life of sorts in the south-west (the previous Easter, he and a group of friends cycled ten miles to the East Devon Point-to-Point, inflaming a lifelong passion for horses and gambling) while the Cranford Club offered tennis, squash – and girls, all of which was brought to an end by his arrival at Sherborne.

If one discounts his enormous ears, Dempster had developed into a rather good-looking young man, with a trim, tall frame, deep brown eyes and a lean face cracked by a thin-lipped smile. One Diana Tremlett certainly had a crush on him in the summer of 1954 and thought him 'very attractive and totally charming'. She continues: 'He definitely had "it" as far as the girls were concerned, and was always the centre of attention. He was somehow a bit different from all of us, a bit exotic.' And as such, he was not best suited to the rigours of public school life in the austerity years. At Sherborne, the day started with a cold shower and there was an emphasis on the cadet corps, new boys fagged for their seniors and you were beaten if you failed to tip your boater, or 'basher', to a passing prefect.

Dempster got off to a bad start, explaining that he couldn't be confirmed in the Church of England, as his father had even forbidden his christening. He enjoyed the sporting life – again making both first elevens – but in other respects was a far from model pupil. Although his old rugby coach, Major Michael Earls-Davis remembered him as 'quite one of the best wing-forwards I ever had in the Colts', it is said that he grew his nails long so that he could scratch opponents' faces in the scrum.* Another Old Shirburnian, the late architect Christopher Bowerbank, claimed to have enjoyed secret kisses with him in the study they shared. But since they were not in the same year – and Sherborne had strict rules against boys of different ages socialising – this seems unlikely. Besides, there were plenty of other ways for Dempster to get into trouble; and for which he was frequently thrashed.

There was his cigarette supply business, for example, and his catering concern. (Asking for a primus stove for Christmas, he then used it to cook sausages bought in town, which he would sell to the hungry boys.) There were his trips to Cheltenham Races, and his unhealthy obsession with the mid-market broadsheets' pseudonymously-authored gossip columns – Paul Tanfield in the *Mail* and William Hickey in the *Express* – which he devoured every day. (The former was named after the *Mail*'s building in Edinburgh, the latter after a celebrated 19th-century rake and memoirist.) Above all, there was his attitude.

Erika says that, after six of the best, he once asked:

---

* This may have been an early manifestation of a later affectation, when Dempster allowed the nail on his left little finger to grow long, in the 'brahmin' style of his native India, to denote that he did no work.

'Can't I have some more?' And though intelligent and possessed of an amazing memory – he could put a name to the face of all 625 pupils within three weeks – he showed no interest in lessons. 'He had clearly come from a background where he'd had no discipline,' says Jeremy Cox, who was in the same house. 'He simply refused to conform, and had no fear of authority. He just went his own way. He was always being caught out of bounds. I suppose he was uncontrollable.' But, Cox remembers him as 'the only special person in the year above' and 'very tough'. In one epic boxing match – 'it should have been stopped' – he watched Dempster 'battle on, covered in blood. But he wouldn't let anyone get the better of him.'

'Nigel always stood out,' agrees the actor Charles Collingwood, who was two years below him. 'He cut a dash, and I had the impression that some of the staff lived in fear of him. The vents in his coat blew out more than other boys', his brolley was more tightly furled.' There was a custom that one's basher should not be too pristine – 'like a dweeb from the school shop' – but Dempster took this to extremes, altogether detaching the rim from the crown.

Not that he was immune to old-school snobbery: Erika recalls her brother, already mortified by their father's great age, being 'acutely embarrassed' one sports day, when their parents arrived in a car that he considered *declassé*. Generally, though, he tended to adapt Sherborne's ethos to his own requirements. 'This was at the height of the Cold War,' says Collingwood. There was still National

Service conscription until the early Sixties. 'And we all fully expected to be sent to freeze in a trench somewhere. So, without ever explaining what it meant, the masters were always telling us that the point of the place was to turn out "chaps" who would later run the show.' Dempster, says Collingwood, 'was one hell of a chap', just not the Sherborne sort – as he put beyond doubt the day he organised a mass refusal to eat school lunch.

It was the final straw. In the summer of 1958, the headmaster told Demy his son (who had only convincingly passed one 'O' Level, in Maths) would not be welcome back – a complication that Dempster senior could well do without. Having retired and finally left India in 1956, he and Topsy had initially installed themselves in a hotel in Belsize Park, London. Here they were close to both Erika's lodgings and the flat of Pam and her first husband. However, early the next year, the odd couple had decided to drive round Spain for six weeks, with a possible view to emigration. On the return journey, the ferry stopped at Jersey, and this was decisive for their future: Demy decided it would be the ideal place to spend the rest of his days, free from income tax in Britain, and where he could swim in the sea and play all the golf he wanted.

Topsy, however, was far from enamoured with the island, the games of bridge which she didn't play, the rounds of parties and endless drinking in which everyone drowned their sorrows or boredom. Nor was she impressed by the type of house that Demy thought within their means. She elected to stay on in London, he moved to a guesthouse in St Aubin, and until his death in 1983, they shuttled between the two.

After four years, Topsy took a short-lease flat in Hampstead – and stayed there as a controlled tenant until her death in 1999. At first, she would reluctantly spend five months a year in Jersey, taking in the winter, and Demy would come to London for his 90 days' tax-free allowance over the summer. (He stayed with one or other daughter, to comply with the revenue regulations forbidding cohabitation with his spouse.) Eventually, though, Topsy reduced her visits to two months a year, generally around Easter and Christmas, when their offspring came too.

Given such lengthy separations, it is unsurprising that the Dempsters were never a close family, but Nigel's heartlessness would become quite shocking. At two dinners in the early Seventies, he told them all that he never wanted to see them again, and attacked his father for his distant parenting. And though he seems to have eventually developed respect and even affection for Demy – who became an occasional golfing partner – his aversion to his mother grew to such an extent that, when he was dying (though, at this stage, perhaps deranged by his illness) he told Erika that he had 'always hated' her.

To her own end, his mother adored him – keeping every picture of him she found in the press, and every word written by or about him. Erika says, 'She lived vicariously through him,' and he found it 'distasteful'. Pam remembers an occasion when the aged and ailing

Topsy was in hospital on her birthday and 'Nigel arrived, tossed a present on her bed and departed to the taxi that he had kept running'. In his pomp, a sliver of conscience pricked him to telephone her once a week and – accompanied by one or other sister as a diversion – to take her for birthday lunches. But he made no attempt to visit her in the final weeks of her life, and was not present for her demise.

Still, at 16, the errant schoolboy needed his parents and they had a duty to him; so the irate Demy decided that Nigel should move in with his mother. The boy had already stayed in Belsize Park in the holidays – by day, taking a temporary job in the gentlemen's socks department at Harrods, and by night becoming very friendly with Priscilla, the daughter of the house. Until September he was to attend a 'crammer' in Kensington, called Davies Tutors, in the hope of obtaining some more 'O' Levels.

He managed to scrape through his English Literature and Language exams – and perhaps should be congratulated, given that his teacher committed suicide midway through the course. (Dempster rather luridly claimed to have discovered him swinging from a beam in the classroom.) But as far as his future was concerned, he laid much more important foundations – for it was at the crammer that Nigel was to meet a very special sort of student. These boys, also rejects from fee-paying schools, had elder sisters who were holding debutante parties and balls – and Dempster was to be invited.

***

That, at least, was one version of his progress peddled by the grown-up Dempster. In interviews, he also said he joined the deb circuit when he became a trainee insurance broker at Lloyds of London. Whichever is correct, having wangled that job through Neil Robertson, the father of a Davies Tutors friend (definitively citing both 1 November 1958 and 1 January 1959 as his starting date) he lost it after extending a holiday without permission.

As the Fifties came to a close, Dempter's ambitions had not yet turned to journalism – but the profession was very much on the mind of playwright John Osborne. Sore from the press scrutiny given to the break-up of his second marriage, the author of *Look Back In Anger* staged a musical, *The World of Paul Slickey* (combining the names of Paul Tanfield and William Hickey), which prophetically featured a vain, amoral gossip columnist with an aristocratic wife. And while the play closed after a short run, never to re-open, the dramatist was revenged on his tormentors when the third Mrs Osborne, the journalist Penelope Gilliatt, wrote a polemic about diarists for the fortnightly *Queen* magazine, which had become the Chelsea Set's Bible since Jocelyn Stevens bought and re-vamped it in 1957.

'They go where they are not asked,' she wrote in 'The Friendless Ones'. 'They live in a world which exists only in their fertile imaginations; they are supplied with information by your friends; they have a language, a code, an attitude as unreal as the news they deal in.' As for the hapless victim of these ogres, 'like any blackmailed person, he often develops a curious and hopeless sense of intimacy with his tormentor, so that he is even insane enough to think that "off the record" has some meaning.'

This spate of invective had a remarkable effect, unimaginable now that 'Society' counts for so little and glossy journalism is so tepid. But *Queen* was a magazine like no other before or since, emblematic in its heyday of a swinging Britain where the old and new orders were beginning to collide and collude. In its writing, it was often a self-regarding pastiche of the American 'new journalism'. In its coverage of anyone who was anyone, it could be cocksure, knowing, occasionally pointless. ('We thought we were frightfully clever,' says Drusilla Beyfuss, an early features staffer.) But however smug, it was always stylish and sharp.

Horrified by what he read in this smart magazine, the *Daily Mail*'s proprietor, the second Viscount Rothermere, 'killed' Paul Tanfield – briefly replacing 'him' with the affable Quentin Crewe, who wrote a dismal good-news diary. Clearly, the *Mail* was not yet right for Dempster's greatest incarnation. Although he would later claim that Lloyds had been 'just a bigger boarding school' and he a contemptible 'clone in a three-piece suit and bowler hat', he immediately found another position in the City, this time as a 'blue button' at the Stock Exchange. However, here, by his own account, he had some sort of epiphany. 'These Hoorah [sic] Henrys shouldn't have a right to exist,' the born-again

meritocrat would later say of his contemporaries from
Eton, Harrow and Winchester. He wanted to work in an
environment where talent was the key qualification – or
at least the talent to socialise.

In that context, the forays into finance were mere
footnotes to his main business. Although Dempster
remained a keen sportsman – playing rugby in Richmond
at weekends, jogging every morning before breakfast – he
had also discovered the louche life. He became a regular
at a Cromwell Road drinking club, for example, where
his crony was Lord Valentine Thynne. And from 1959,
for several years, he was a semi-professional partygoer;
attending all the traditional highlights of the English
Season – Ascot, Cowes, Henley – and specialising in the
strange anachronism of 'coming out'.

These annual rounds of champagne-fuelled festivities
started officially with the Royal Academy Summer Show
in late April – or less formally, with Queen Charlotte's
Ball in the first week of May – and ended with grouse-
shooting's Glorious Twelfth. For its younger participants,
it was part mating ritual, part rite of passage, and served
to 'launch' the daughters of the upper and upper-middle
classes into Society – a network that in one of his sourer
moments, Dempster recalled was full of 'old snobs who
were ripe to be taken'.

In 1959, the deb circuit should have been on its last legs.
The previous year, the presentation of debutantes at Court
had been abolished, the Queen thinking such a socially
divisive ceremony gave a bad impression of her modern

monarchy (and her sister Margaret saying, 'We had to put a stop to it – every tart in London was getting in'). Meanwhile, the majority of young people considered the scene irredeemably 'square'; whether nurtured on Bill Haley or Beat poetry, they were heralding the start of the permissive society.

Yet the Season's social whirl – oiled by the 'never had it so good' economy of Prime Minister Harold Macmillan – was giddier than it had been for decades. The million-aire's daughter Rose Dugdale, later an IRA terrorist, described her 1959 ball as 'one of those pornographic affairs which cost about what 60 old-age pensioners re-ceive in six months'. According to Dempster, there were at least two cocktail parties every night, and at least three balls every weekend. 'You could choose which county you wanted to go and dance in,' he once said. 'All it required was a white tie and tails.'

Dempster claimed to have stolen his evening dress. His morning coat would come from the wardrobe of Erika's first husband (and last him a lifetime). Of other cloth-ing items, he advised his new friend Lord Antony Rufus-Isaacs that 'you only needed two – one to wear and one being cleaned'. The Marquess of Reading's second son, a year younger than his mentor, would eventually become his landlord, but for now Dempster relied on his own family. First he moved from his mother's hotel to Erika's lodgings, in an upper maisonette in Frognal Gardens. When Erika's landlord died and the widowed landlady emigrated, the Dempsters bought the flat on a short lease and it was originally shared by Nigel, both his sisters and Pam's first husband.

After a family conference convened by Demy to discuss the discovery of his son's unpaid bookmakers' bills (at a time when off-course betting was still illegal) Dempster's luck turned. His father not only saw off the bookies in person – pointing out that their debtor was underage – but agreed that, while his son remained in regular employment, he would guarantee the rent on a small flat in Nell Gwynne House, the apartment block on Sloane Avenue. Dempster's £6 a week wage was supplement by £4 from his father – an arrangement that lasted for a couple of years.

Following his disillusionment with the Stock Exchange, not to mention his actual dismissal, Dempster worked as a catering assistant with Searcy's, and for a while as a door-to-door vacuum-cleaner salesman. (Legend has it that he spread dust all over the comedian Frankie Howerd's carpet, was unable to suck it up, but was still invited by the lascivious entertainer to stay for a drink.) And when he was not on call, 'I got up late and took the bus to Harrods. I had my shoes polished on the lower ground floor, thence to the health juice bar, then down to the main lobby – to the bank – where by one o'clock you were guaranteed to meet at least twenty debs. That's how I got to know the lie of the land.'

However, by the time he was 19 – and coincidentally, after reading an article on public relations in *Queen* magazine – Dempster had found a job as general factotum to the outrageous Earl of Kimberley, one-time war hero and PR man for among others Smirnoff, the new vodka brand, and the film-maker Samuel Bronston, then famed for *El Cid* and *King of Kings*.

At Kimberley Associates, he might be feeding the meters, or organising press conferences for actors at Pinewood Studios. One of his jobs was to cultivate the press, whose diary columns were useful for keeping clients in the public eye; and, as he learned at Kimberley's feet, stories about one's circle could raise some useful cash. Excited by his daily contact with scribblers and stars, Dempster was about to step out on his road to perdition. As much a hostage to the beau monde as its denizens were to the 'friendless ones', he realised that his gregarious nature and burgeoning address book could give him more than a freeloading life; he could turn it to profit.

By his own account, it was during Cowes Week of 1961 that the *Express* proprietor, Lord Beaverbrook, suggested he should contribute to the William Hickey column – then so vital a component of the mighty paper that it dominated page three. However, it was not until January 1962 that he sold his first story – about his pal Sir William Piggott-Brown, the champion amateur jockey, inheriting £750,000 on his twenty-first birthday.

Over the years, the public would hear much more of that particular character, but for now Dempster was only assembling his cast. Simultaneously, he was forming a rat pack, running with a renegade set of hip young hacks whose degree of prosperity ranged from the impecunious

American Jon Bradshaw – later long-term lover of US *Vogue*'s editor, Anna Wintour – via the should-be baronet Anthony 'Uninvited' Haden-Guest, to the noble Patrick Lichfield.

The fifth Earl of Lichfield, a middle-distant cousin of the Queen, was newly out of the Guards and hoping to make a career as a professional photographer. Before long, he would achieve that, becoming almost a parody of the bouffant snapper-playboy. (Paid in crates of champagne, he would also become one of Dempster's greatest sources, not least of royal stories.) But for now, he was knocking on doors – and Dempster was answering Kimberley's.

***

They no longer make them like the Earl of Kimberley, who was already well on the way to becoming the most-married man in the peerage in 1960. At Dempster's age, he had been an undergraduate at Cambridge, but his studies were curtailed when he got drunk in a nightclub and 'accidentally enlisted in the Grenadier Guards'. During the liberation of Brussels, he captured so much champagne that he always kept a case in his tank, and finished the war both a lieutenant and an alcoholic.

A bobsleigher for Great Britain, in the 1950s, Kimberley also acquired a reputation as a danger on the roads. He was frequently fined, once tried to drive up the steps of the Grand Hotel in Brighton, and eventually killed a pedestrian whom he claimed not to have seen crossing

Piccadilly. At the same time, he was running his PR company, representing such clients at Les Ambassadeurs gaming club – which re-launched in the old Rothschild house off Park Lane – and such stars as Gregory Peck, Robert Mitchum and 'that bald bugger' Yul Brynner. At first a Liberal in the House of Lords, he advised the electorate to vote Conservative, and was sacked from his party. Joining the Tories, he once declared: 'Queers have been the downfall of all the great empires.'

And women of many great men. Kimberley's first marriage, in 1945, was to Diana Legh, daughter of the Court official Sir Piers, whom he met on a blind date at the Ritz. The wedding took place at St George's Chapel, even though the young officer already knew he had blundered. 'I couldn't stop it,' he said later, 'because the King and Queen were there, and I was in my best uniform.' Within a year, he 'gave the butler a note to give to her saying that it wasn't going to work out, [so] since her mother was sailing for America that night why didn't she go too?'

Number two ended Kimbereley's playboy period. He would weekend at the Deauville races, join John Aspinall's all-night semi-legal chemmy sessions and bed any women he could. He claimed to have succeeded with Eartha Kitt – and to have been rebuffed by Princess Margaret – before his 1949 wedding to Carmel Dunnett, one of the Australian boxer Mickey Maguire's five daughters. (He met her through her elder sibling, a previous conquest who had married Lord Beaverbrook's second son.)

They were divorced in 1952, and the third countess

was a Suffolk farmer's wife, whom the earl encountered over the horseflesh at Newmarket. Invited to recuperate from polio at Kimberley, his seat in Norfolk, 'she never moved out'. Next up was Maggie Simons, a 23-year-old model and daughter of a cafe owner. She refused to sleep with Kimberley until he proposed – which he did within a week. Married in 1961, 'we both drank a fair amount and had fearful fights'.

Two more wives were to follow, but by then Dempster had long left his employ. During his time there, he had learned some bad habits: not least Kimberley's fondness for the bottle. He had sharpened others, watching the swells over the gaming tables at Les Ambassadeurs. Most importantly for his future, he had cleared some broad new social avenues. He called his time with Kimberley 'a training course in social climbing'; his apparently open manner, quick wit and cheeky tongue endeared him to Beaverbrook's clan, the Aitkenses, as well as to the Soameses and many other grandees.

'What you have to remember,' says Antony Rufus-Isaacs, 'is that before Nigel even became a gossip columnist, he already knew all the people he would later write about, and for the most part they liked him.' He sometimes liked them, too, and adored Rufus-Isaacs' marchioness mother (who gave her dogs such names as 'Toilet', 'Pardon', 'Fire' and 'Taxi'). What's more, they liked to be liked. To their faces, at least, Dempster showed none of the resentment they might fear from a have-not. They were generous to him; he was their pet.

'It never occurred to the people whose parties I went to that I was any different from those who introduced me,' he would remember. 'I got into that stream and stayed there simply by being amusing, charming and nice.' It was a seductive life, where all you paid for was 'the cleaning of your clothes'. And that, he said, 'was the beginning of my ruin, because I discovered free food, free drink and free women – all the fs.' Including fun: 'I quickly realized that money equals fun, and I didn't see why I shouldn't go to debs' parties. What I lacked in "background", I made up for in enthusiasm... I think they found it refreshing to meet someone with no money whatsoever.'

His acceptance may not have been quite so straightforward as he claimed. The obituarist who reported that Dempster bought a selection of old school ties to ease his social passage misunderstood his motives. The story dates from his spell at Lloyds, when Dempster would change his neckwear to ingratiate himself with whichever broker he needed to underwrite his business. However, he did tell this writer that, if he lacked a ticket to a ball, he would gatecrash it by walking up the hotel steps with a glass of champagne already in his hand – 'which always fooled the doormen'. He had a delightful arrangement with the band leader Joe Loss, so that when he waltzed by with a girl, he would say 'Good evening, Joe', and Loss would reply 'My lord.' And whether or not he provided the information, when a photographer repeatedly described Dempster in picture captions as 'son of the shipping line chief', he made no attempt to correct it.

In his mind, there probably was a distinction between private invitations and opportunities to gather gossip, and he trimmed his sail accordingly. Colleagues from his early days as a down-table diarist are adamant that he let it be understood he was an Old Etonian. They remember, too, that when he covered a coming-out dance at Paul Getty's Surrey mansion, Sutton Place – lent by the grateful client to his mistress-decorator's daughter Penny Kitson – Dempster was smuggled through the gates in the boot of Patrick Lichfield's car. But Rufus-Isaacs prefers the story that, if asked where he went to school, his friend would reply 'Harrods'. 'Nigel,' he says, 'would never have risked the shame of being found out. He didn't need to pretend, because he was accepted.'

Perhaps Dempster shielded his friend from some of his grosser misdemeanours. But to be fair, a total charlatan would soon have been rumbled. The press at this time took an almost embarrassing interest in reporting the scene, and in perpetuating it. *The Times* published a monthly-updated list of private dances, which competed with such charity balls as the Pineapple and Pied Piper, the Red Cross and the Silver Rose. In what might now be called brand-reinforcement, the social editor of *Queen* magazine, Betty Kenward provided would-be hostesses with a list of suitable girls and escorts. Given the dynamics of debbery, the latter were always in short supply and unlike the natty Nigel, often rather gauche.

While the papers ran annual features on who would be the Deb (or male Delight) of the Year, one group of young men published a yearly form-guide, disguised as a novel, which assessed the new crop. For five guineas, subscribers could learn if a girl was TT ('The Tops') or TB (the reverse). CB meant 'Crashing Bore', AD 'Appearance Deceptive', TTB 'Too, Too Brainy' and L simply 'Limpid'. Dance invitations were rated A or RQ ('Accept' or 'Refuse Quickly'), AYOR ('At Your Own Risk') and OIH ('Only If Hungry').

There were a host of ancillary industries, too. Portrait photographers, band leaders, milliners and dressmakers were booked months in advance. In 1960, Lord Lichfield's sister, Lady Elizabeth Anson, invented party planning with her inventively titled company, Party Planners. Meanwhile, a cash-strapped dowager could top up her pension by 'bringing out' a parvenue – charging £1000 to obtain the right introductions and lend her London house for a gathering – while enterprising debs' delights could supplement their income by selling pictures and reports to the press.

SHINE
The Socially Mobile Sixties

By 1963, Kimberley had gone into five years of tax exile, and the newly unemployed Dempster was scraping a living from giving gossip tips to the *Daily Express* as a 'casual'. A common sight on the back stairs, he would pick up his five-pound fees from the cashier's office in Fleet Street, where Beaverbrook's black-glass Art Deco palace bore proud witness to the paper's four-million-plus circulation. Without a steady income, though, he had to move around. Pitching up at the tiny Kensington flat of his sister Erika, newly separated from her first husband, 'he said he'd be there for ten days and stayed for ten months'. Dempster slept on the sofa, only separated from his sister's bed by a thin curtain; and since Erika was secretly having an affair with her married boss, 'his erratic comings and goings were a nightmare for me'.

Her brother, though, was well placed for his work. Lichfield had also visited the *Express*, and secured a free-lance agreement from Robin Esser, the editor of the Hickey page. For obvious reasons, the diary wanted pictures of well-bred dolly birds, so it would pay the costs of the studio in Lichfield's Campden Hill Road house if he could deliver a quota ('and preferably,' says Esser, 'wearing Mary Quant's white boots'). Dempster, who was now living nearby, was charged with writing the captions, and both relied on prowling the deb scene to locate their prey.

By now, Dempster was becoming ubiquitous. He was a dinner guest at Number Eleven Downing Street, when the Chancellor's daughter, Caroline Maudling, was launched; and at Number Ten for a drinks party given in honour of Harold Macmillan's granddaughter, Anne Faber. And if the whole notion sounds faintly ridiculous at the dawn of the Swinging Sixties – teenagers playing at being adults in stuffed shirts and evening gowns – Julian Fellowes re-members it still going strong at that decade's dusk. In his novel *Past Imperfect*, set in 1968, he writes:

'In the forty years that followed, that decade has been hijacked by the voice of the Liberal Tyranny... and they have no conscience in holding up the values of the pop revolution as the whole truth, but they are either deceiving or deceived.' What was genuinely unusual about the era, he continues, was not 'a bunch of guitar players smoking dope' but that 'it faced both ways'. In Fellowes' opinion, 'the girls who wouldn't kiss on the first date, the boys who were not dressed without a tie, those mothers who only left the house in hat and gloves, those fathers wearing bowlers on their way to the City. These were all as much a part of the Sixties as the side of it so constantly revived in television documentaries.'

But though post-presentation debbery would even survive the year of revolutions, hairline cracks in the Seasonal edifice had been spreading for quite some time. The Saddle Room, London's first 'disco', had opened in Park Lane in 1961, and was soon followed by such clubs as Le Discothèque in Wardour Street, and the military-themed Garrison Room in the basement of Les Ambassadeurs. At Queen's ice-rink, debs could be seen skating in their officer-boyfriends' striped mess trousers. And there was a dangerously democratic trend afoot at the bigger dances, whereby guests were asked to bring a change of casual clothes: at midnight, the band was dismissed, and a sound system hooked up; the girls and boys retired, and reappeared in jeans and T-shirts to twist and frug until dawn.

Dempster may have been a hell-raiser – the PR Liz Brewer remembers him riding into a nightclub on a motorcycle with one of her cousins – but he was never a fashion follower. 'He was more of a pinstripe man,' says Anthony Haden-Guest. 'It's a style that's still very popular.' Similarly, he was a never really a pop music man – Beethoven and opera, picked up from Topsy, were more to his taste – but when an opportunity came to profit from the new craze, he thought it a better bet than his current precarious profession. John Mills, the owner of Les Ambassadeurs, an associate of Lord Kimberley and the father of one of Dempster's old friends, had expanded into New York, bought the famous El Morocco nightclub – which had just moved to new premises – and installed in it a copy of his Garrison Room. Dempster was offered a job there, and later claimed to be manager (though others have described his role as greeter, or even doorman).

While in Manhattan, he met the decorator Nicholas Haslam, then working on *Vogue* magazine. And though 'Nigel was playing the public schoolboy and I was determined not to', the pair became lifelong friends. 'But he was funnier in those days,' says Haslam. 'It was before he began to breathe the same air as the great and good, and he used to mock them.' Gossip columns were avidly read in New York then, with people vying for a mention from Cholly Knickerbocker or Carol Bjorkman, and Haslam thinks Dempster would later model his upbeat style on theirs – 'although he introduced a darker side, dealing in illicit relationships like the Hollywood magazines'.

As for the club, it was not a great success. The original El Morocco, which started life as a Prohibition speakeasy, had played host to Marilyn Monroe and Marlene Dietrich. Jackie Bouvier visited as both a Kennedy and an Onassis. Cary Grant was a regular and Humphrey Bogart was banned for life. But when the operation moved from 3rd to 2nd Avenue, although its trademark décor was recreated, it failed to capture the in-crowd's imagination. Dempster, cox-and-boxing in a cheap hotel room, must have found the experience dispiriting. And if it's true that he was mistakenly served with draft papers, he had an added incentive to leave the States. Whichever, he did not return empty-handed, having secured a contract to provide features about the English aristocracy for the now-defunct *Status* magazine.

Back in London, he was now hanging out with such sharp young men as Colin Slater and Ian Heath, and had acquired something of a nickname. The three would dress in identical shades and Minoxes for the races and Heath always gave Dempster a berth in his father's flat at Cowes, above Lord Beaverbrook's sail loft. But they never let him forget that, for all the suits from Dougie Hayward, he was not quite the gentleman. To them, as another of the Cowes crew, Michael 'Dupraved' Dupree remembers, he was known as 'Flash'.

Although he endured the ribbing with good grace, the effect may have been to galvanise him. Back on the Hickey desk as a staffer, the journalist Glenys Roberts, who crossed paths with him there, suspects that 'he was a little jealous of all those Old Etonians, which made him more determined to succeed.' Peter McKay, who joined the *Express* in 1964, recalls him saying that he went into the gossip industry 'to nail the type of bastards who were rude to waiters'. Although at this stage Dempster still covered his tracks ('for at least two years, when he rang people up he claimed to be "James Hamilton from *Queen*",' says his then-colleague Colin Mackenzie) his work still became his life, or vice versa.

Where women were concerned, he didn't have any problems. There have been unkind interpretations put on Dempster's penchant for well-off women (not helped by labelling himself the 'founder-president of Fortune Hunters Inc') but he never let himself be kept, or kept from his curious vocation. He eventually earned envious salaries, which he needn't have wasted on horses. In McKay's view, 'he may just have been attracted to that sort of girl' – and one can only applaud his taste, as Carolyne Christie – the racehorse trainer's daughter, who was a niece of the Marquess of Zetland – was followed by Audrey Hoare of the banking family.

Christie, whose family home was Jervaulx Abbey in Yorkshire, dated him in 1964 and thought him 'very glamorous and dashing – much more sophisticated than the other boys on the deb scene'. She loved his 'photographic memory and the anecdotes that he used to embellish'. Having no gossip to impart, she liked to talk about history and horses with him, and remembers how once, when he brought her home at breakfast time, her father said: 'You can have my daughter, but not my *Sporting Life*.' But she never thought of their romance – which ended with his sojourn in New York – as being 'serious'.

Hoare, on the other hand, had to turn down his offer of marriage during their three-year affair. In 1966, after seeing her photograph at the *Express*, Dempster rang her up, asked about her interests – which included the Mamas and Papas singing group – and later posted 'California Dreaming' and 'Monday Monday' through her letter box. 'He was so sophisticated,' she says, 'and amusing.' But dangerous, too: 'I never told my parents that he was a gossip columnist – I always said he wrote for *Status* magazine – and I was always very careful what I said in front of him.'

So careful indeed that, rather than split up with him, she decided to go around the world, leaving their relationship in the air. ('I was scared he might write some-thing about me.') They agreed to meet in Paris on her return, to take stock. 'But,' she says, 'it was a disaster. The chemistry had gone', if not the friendship. Apart from a hiatus in the Eighties, when Dempster betrayed a con-fidence in print, the relationship lasted his lifetime – as it did with Anna Wintour, who he escorted through the foothills of the glossy realm that she would one day make her own.

A myth has grown up that Dempster 'went out' with the 16-year-old Wintour when he was 25. Again, our hero did not help by telling a very amusing story in which Charles Wintour – then editor of the *Evening Standard* – did not approve of his daughter's liaisons and kept a beady eye on the pair. In this yarn, old man Wintour would creep up on them in his suede shoes; and one night, while Dempster dallied with his teenage girlfriend on her drawing-room sofa, he glanced at the curtains, only to see the telltale (and occupied) Hush Puppies sticking out from beneath...

***

Some stories really are too good to check. 'I don't think Nigel ever came to the house,' says Wintour. 'And – I can't make this more clear – there was nothing romantic about our relationship. I think he was trying to take care of me at a certain level.' She calls Dempster 'sweet', 'loyal' and 'a very good friend' who used to 'squire me around for openings… and seemed pleased for the company'. In fact, it was through him that she met Jon Bradshaw and became an addition to their roguish battalion. But her memory can be 'hazy' now, and she forgets the group's more outrageous exploits. 'I know there was a lot of drinking,' she says. 'But I was always the first to leave. I had to get up and go to work in the mornings. Because they were freelancers, they could wake up later.'

When they did, they went for a jog. They also compensated for their dissipation with a furious energy. After grouping and regrouping in various Chelsea flats, by 1967 a nucleus emerged. Dempster, Bradshaw and Haden-Guest became tenants of Antony Rufus-Isaacs, first in Ennismore Gardens and then Oakley Gardens. In and out of their sphere passed all sorts of characters – from the ludicrous Hooray underwriter Rupert Deen, to the Cambridge medical student-turned-banker-turned-psychiatrist Garth Wood (with whom some say Dempster was 'infatuated'). And none of them behaved very well. 'We were slaying, raping and pillaging,' says the landlord in a lurid turn of phrase. 'Girls going from one bed to another, it was very decadent. Our lives were in the red of the rev counter all the time.'

Haden-Guest remembers the 'post-austerity exuberance and confidence' of those years: 'It seemed that our generation had filled all the slots – photographers, directors, playwrights – and I remember wondering if it would ever be like that again.' Having formed a 'Monday Club' – that met on the first Tuesday of every month at San Lorenzo, the chic new restaurant on Beauchamp Place – the Dempster gang was eventually forced to find a fresh venue after Lord Lichfield had to be restrained from mounting the stairs on his motorbike. 'But we were thrown out of everywhere,' continues Rufus-Isaacs. Their motto was: 'There's no point spending forty quid to take out a girl, when you can spend it on yourself.'

While a hipper London drifted from the Ad Lib club, where the Beatles held court, to the UFO, where Pink Floyd freaked out, these King's Road cavaliers would treat their girlfriends at places 'where you could get out for a fiver'. For lunch, favourites included r's and Alexander's, the restaurant beneath Mary Quant's shop, run by her husband Alexander Plunket-Greene. By night, the crowd moved on to Club del Aretusa, Sibylla's or the Bistrotheque (an offshoot of Fun Unlimited, the band-booking agency run by Rufus-Isaacs). And strangely enough, as Dempster plied his trade, he became a man to know. '[That group] may have benefited from the fruits of snobbery, like Lichfield,' says Haden-Guest, 'but they weren't snobs themselves.' And

Dempster was very much at home among them. Puffed by his friends in *Queen*, which had become brasher, but still very successful, Dempster also contributed to the magazine, writing or directing some of its iconic features.

In 1967, for example, he worked with Jon Bradshaw on a picture story called 'You Can Judge a Man By the Company He Keeps'. The idea had been to shoot a variety of cliques, but in the studio fluid organisation – and social barriers – resulted in a hopeless mix-up, with good eggs and bad hats, toffs and trade all in together. Comedian Ronnie Corbett was in the same photograph as the Bishop of London and satirist Jonathan Miller. The moral crusader Mary Whitehouse shared a spread with hairdresser Justin de Villeneuve, deejay David Jacobs, villainous Robert Maxwell and – of course – Sir William Piggott-Brown.

Queen added a question mark to the headline, and turned the piece into social commentary. But then, it liked to play tricks. The following year, in the Valentine's issue, the magazine ran a collection of Dempster interviews with eligible young men – including Piggott-Brown again, and the hippyish publishing heir Michael Pearson – then tacked onto it a competition to 'Win a Millionaire'. Unbeknown to Lichfield, who was asked to provide a self-portrait, he was the prize, at least for the duration of a photographic session and dinner. The first he heard of it was when his mother phoned to tell him he'd gone too far. Asked how, the dowager replied: 'You have raffled yourself,' and hung up.

The ragging was more vicious in the Hickey office, and coarser. When Glenys Roberts' husband phoned from the lobby to say he had arrived to drive her home, Dempster said, 'She's already gone off with a big black man.' (That caused a certain *froideur*.) But his worst behaviour was reserved for the team's fall guy, David 'Panda' Pitman. He would be rapped with rulers, and hung out of the window over Shoe Lane, his typewriter and notes having preceded him. He was bound to his chair with parcel tape and had waste bins crammed on his head. On one occasion, glue was tipped into his hair; on another, while conducting a telephone interview with Prince Richard of Gloucester, he was turned upside down – and to his credit, continued the conversation.

Pitman retired to the Isle of Mull to run a grocery store. 'But I think he enjoyed it,' says his colleague Geoffrey Levy. And indeed there was fun to be had. In 1967, when Joe Coral began accepting bets on the Miss World competition, the inveterate gambler Colin Mackenzie was sent out to study the form in person, report back that Miss Peru was his favourite. Collecting £300 from the editorial floor, he placed the bet at Coral's office (handily situated beneath the *Express* building) while others in the Hickey team rang round the judges to sing the praises of Miss Peru. As it was, she romped home.

Such Wodehousian high jinks were part of the camaraderie fostered on the twelve-man desk – like the contest to be 'Lead Machine', an honour often claimed by Dempster over Mackenzie. Today, Mackenzie can't remember any of his friend's triumphs, though he does recall some of his own: the Tower of London warden who was doing bed-and-breakfast for American girls on the quiet, say, or the stick-up at the Casanova casino, where an oblivious brigadier called 'Banco!'

Then there was the story, which both of them worked on, of the Treasury minister Harold Lever, who was spotted playing backgammon at the Palace Hotel in Gstaad – and losing thousands – while currency regulations forbade ordinary Britons from taking more than £50 out of the country. That one was 'spiked' after Harold Wilson made threatening noises about withdrawing the paper's access to the parliamentary lobby.

Seldom, however, were the scoops of such a high calibre. Under a succession of editors, Hickey depended on titled heads for a faint aura of glamour: their births and couplings crowded its column. Even the daily horoscope was penned by 'Lord Luck'. The Royal Family's outings were closely monitored, with Princess Margaret's rackety marriage being covered in deft code. But since pretty girls from the very top drawer were hard to come by, the daughters of estate agents and stockbrokers often filled the picture slot ('For Veronica and Alicia, life is fascinating').

By the end of the Sixties, Prince Michael's progress on the British bobsleighing team was still considered worth noting, but the decade had made some impact. Greater attention was paid to Hollywood – say, Burton buying Taylor the Krupp diamond – and the appearance of the 'jet set' brought in more news from the Continent, the doings of Gunter Sachs and the Cresta Run set being regularly relayed from St Moritz. At the same time, Dempster quoted and promoted his friends. When he filed a page for the 'August Capitals' series from Long Island, New York, he name-checked his host Nick Simunek. During a postal strike, he reported on Lichfield's new scooter-delivery service. (The picture, naturally supplied by Lichfield, featured Stetson-wearing Jon Bradshaw perched on a Honda 'monkey bike', handing a letter to the leggy Felicity Cadbury.)

But even without the PR and the tip fees at Dempster's disposal, 'a lot of people just liked being in the gossip columns, or passing on information,' says Rufus-Isaacs. 'It made them feel important. So Nigel would be invited to parties by hostesses who might say behind his back, "I can't imagine who brought him", but still asked him aside for a quiet word.' Besides, Dempster did a reasonable job of separating the truly private from the seemingly so. Employing the triple standards that every diarist does, he tried not to upset a certain kind of pal, while merrily outraging others. One line he regularly used was 'I'm a professional journalist, not a professional friend.' Unsurprising, then, that some took precautions.

'I was very fond of Nigel' says Lady Elizabeth Anson, who acted as chatelaine at Shugborough, her brother's country pile, 'but I told Patrick I wouldn't sleep under the same roof as him – and when he was invited down, I left.' Even at Staplefield Grange, the Readings' seat in Sussex where Dempster was 'part of the family', certain precautions still applied – for example, Princess Margaret and her photographer husband the Earl of Snowdon could not be exposed to Dempster. As Rufus-Isaacs explains: 'In the late Sixties, Snowdon had restored a house down there. So if they were coming round, I'd get a call from my father telling me not to bring Nigel that weekend.'

***

Because Dempster grasped the rules, however, he could play the game. In 1971, when the American press exposed an affair he had known about – between Snowdon and Rufus-Isaacs' little sister Lady Jacqueline – he was on hand to 'manage' the rebuttal for her. He could bide his time, rather than risk a friendship started seven years earlier at Jacquie's coming-out dance, which she shared with her brother Antony. 'It was his twenty-first,' she says. 'I remember the ladies from the village sewing the yellow silk for the tent, and Antony booked the Kinks to play, although then they were known as the Ravens.'

The siblings' random memories are as much a social commentary as the pages of *Queen*. In London, Dempster borrowed Antony's Bentley. He paid his butler for backstairs tips from Buckingham Palace, where the retainer assisted at banquets. (Beard also ironed Dempster's money.) He stayed with the Reading family for Christmas, and joined in 30-a-side football. In summer, they would drive down to Brighton, rent a speedboat and hop from pier to pier, before lunch at English's.

In the Rufus-Isaacs' circle, journalists and photographers were welcome. It took in not only those born to privilege but fashion designers Ossie Clarke and Bill Gibb, model Pat Booth and Leonard the hairdresser. Says Jacquie: 'They were more exciting to be with than a lot of Establishment types, who were still quite buttoned up. These people were huge fun, they let go, they said and did what they wanted.' And this spirit – more liberal, more egalitarian – was also present on the newsstands. Bookending the decade, *Private Eye* was first published in 1961 by a group of old boys from Shrewsbury School (who would recruit Dempster in 1970). And in 1969, Rupert Murdoch bought the failing *Sun*, turned it into a tabloid and transformed the medium of print.

These matters aside, Dempster had other urgent business. In his late twenties, it was time for him to find a wife. And though his first was rich and aristocratically connected, she was not the obvious choice. He always liked the Audrey Hepburn look – the naughty face, like that of his mother when young – and Emma de Bendern was said to have the naughtiest in London. But she also had an illegitimate daughter. Undeterred, Dempster married her a year after their 1970 meeting – then left within twelve months.

It was Emma's fault. A sexy brunette, she was bequeathed a fortune by her mother's first husband – and given his surname – but she also inherited a wayward streak. On her parents' engagement, her maternal grandfather, the

11th Marquess of Queensbury said to his future brother-in-law: 'My family is mad, and yours is barking. God help the children.'

True to his word, at 17 Emma took up with a handsome, motorcycling, petty criminal called Brian Walsh. By 18, while all her peers were coming out, she was carrying his child. Aged 21, a single mother, she met Dempster at the wedding of Simon Marsden, the photographer and baronet's son. 'It was quite rare for me to be out then,' she recalls. 'Even though I had a nanny, I usually had to stay in to look after my daughter Atalanta. When I met Nigel, I suppose I was a little impressed by him. When he mentioned a horse he fancied for the next day – it was L'Escargot at Cheltenham – I suppose I wanted to show off. I gave him £20, which was a lot in those days, and asked him to put it on for me.'

L'Escargot romped home, and Emma rang Dempster at the office to ask for her winnings. 'You'll have to come out for dinner to collect them,' he said. A breakneck romance followed, with Emma's mother encouraging a wedding that would conceal Atalanta's status. The ceremony was a grand affair, with a reception at Les Ambassadeurs and dinner at Sinatra's favourite London restaurant, Mimmo d'Ischia. Bizarrely, Emma's mother joined the couple in bed for the first night of their marriage and they all cuddled up together.

Dempster moved into Emma's house on the Chelsea-Fulham borders, where the new family was joined by his mother-in-law's peke Bosie (named after Oscar Wilde's boyfriend, the son of an ancestor). There were Lichfield photos of Emma on the walls – and an atmosphere in the air. 'Nigel was a control freak,' she says. 'He always made sure he put the milk order into the empty bottle before I could. He was always agitated, never able to relax, to sit and watch the telly.

'Actually, the whole thing was a serious mistake. I did it for all the wrong reasons – for standing and security – but also for fun. You have to remember that I'd missed out on all that from having a child and from my previously rather shady life, so it was very exciting suddenly to be taken to Ascot and to balls, and to meet all these lords and ladies.' Dempster, too, 'must have thought he'd got a bit of a trophy – I was a countess, you know – but I'm afraid he found he'd bitten off more than he could chew.'

Unfortunately, the marriage had done little to curb the new Mrs Dempster's enthusiasm for unorthodox liaisons. ('I never had the passion for Nigel that he had for me.') Six months after the nuptials, she was at her brother's villa in the south of France, playing hooky with one John Hobbs, a King's Road antiques runner. Halfway through their holiday, Hobbs was rumbled by his wife and rushed home without packing. Emma agreed to bring back his things – but when she arrived at Heathrow, the case containing his clothes failed to appear. Emma arranged that the bag, when found, should be delivered to her neighbour, but this plan went disastrously awry when the overzealous airline staff spotted the label reading

'Mrs Nigel Dempster'. Thinking they were obliging the rising media star, they dispatched it to him in Fleet Street. 'Poor Nigel,' chortles Emma. 'He opened it in front of everyone, only to discover it was packed with Hobbs' clothes.

'I can't remember all the details,' says Emma. 'But I do know there were fisticuffs between Nigel and Hobbs.' Nonetheless, the divorce was painless – 'We never really fell out' – and the pair remained very close. 'I think he loved me more than anyone else in his life, apart from his own daughter.'

Louisa would be the product of Dempster's second marriage, to Lady Camilla Osborne (who also had a baby girl in tow). 'And Nigel used to say that Camilla was in a bad mood for a month whenever we had lunch,' recalls Emma, 'which was about six times a year, usually at San Lorenzo.' To his greater credit, Dempster formed lasting bonds with his ex- and future stepdaughters as much as with Louisa, attending their speech and sports days like the fathers they never really had.

Of his first wife, his second comments: 'Nigel always said he had to marry Emma to get her out of his system.' And now he had to get out of their home. This time, he descended on his other sister Pam, then working in a department of MI6 and living in a modest terraced house off Primrose Hill. However, his patter remained the same. 'The doorbell rang one Sunday morning,' says Pam, 'and there was Nigel. I agreed he could stay three days – but then he started carting in his golf clubs and television. In the end, he stayed three years.'

She remembers her brother as a 'delightful' lodger, who never brought his work home. But sometimes it would pursue him there. In 1973, 'Princess Margaret would phone in the middle of the night, asking where he was,' says Pam. For by then Dempster was well known himself. 'His column was addictive reading,' says Anthony Haden-Guest. 'There had been a class of person who believed the only time you should be in the papers was when you were born, when you married and when you died. So although much of what Nigel wrote may seem innocuous by today's standards, that it was published at all was quite remarkable.'

Famous for writing about people he knew and knowing the people he wrote about, he wasn't just a big gun in the armoury of the re-launched *Daily Mail*, where he fed the particular prejudices of Middle Britain. After a couple of years co-editing the Grovel column with Peter McKay – each contributing three or four paragraphs a fortnight, to which others added – he was also among the main attractions at the snook-cocking *Private Eye*.

While the co-editorship suited both journalists, since each could always blame the other for their indiscretions, it also suited their proprietors and bosses. Though they were often humbled and rumbled in Grovel, Dempster and McKay's moonlighting suited them, since the pair could run items that were less well checked – and generally more scurrilous – in the *Eye* first, whose attitude and funds made it a harder target for libel actions. Before being published in Fleet Street, stories could be floated there and their veracity gauged by the reaction they produced.

But while most of what Dempster printed had some basis in truth, the same could not be said for his conversation. The more he said 'I *promise* you,' recalls Geoffrey Levy, the more you suspended your disbelief. McKay chuckles as he remembers one of Dempster's tactics. 'He would hijack your anecdotes,' he says. 'I used to tell one about the time I was having lunch with Dai Llewellyn when he dashed out. On his return, I asked Dai where he'd been, and he said: "I forgot that I left my secretary tied up in the bath." Well, Dempster claimed it had happened to him – adding the fictitious but convincing detail that Dai's jacket sleeves had been wet up to his elbows!'

Taki Theodoracopulos, who was a close friend and source for 35 years, howls with laughter at Dempster's tall stories. According to the 'Leaky Greeky', or 'Tharally Unscrupulous' – as Dempster called the writer, bon viveur and sportsman – 'the more he insisted that something was true, the less you believed it. "Mister Taki," he would say, "Mister Taki, I assure you this is 100 per cent accurate" – and then tell you that he'd screwed Princess Margaret. Or he'd make up elaborate fantasies about newspaper characters. He did it for the hell of it. You couldn't shut him up. If he heard someone gushing about Lady Whoever, he'd say, "Well she wasn't so wonderful when I was fucking her in a Soho toilet".'

***

This was not, then, a very salubrious scene. But it was of its time and place; and sanctioned by tradition, not entirely charmless. Its spawning ground was Fleet Street and the environs. Ten minutes by taxi from the West End, a brisk walk from the Savoy, taking in the law courts and chambers, the area had an almost mediaeval aspect. This was the lawyers' and journalists' quarter – a smoky, drunken bear pit, where colleagues and rivals, friends and enemies worked and unwound hugger-mugger.

The best-remembered rendezvous now is El Vino's. Run by Geoffrey Van-Hay, a man as spruce and scurrilous as Dempster, this wine bar was where the big beasts went to drink (and women were relegated to a back room). But there were a hundred other watering holes: the King Lud and the Bell, the Tipperary and the Wig and Pen. The Popinjay and the White Swan were known by their nicknames Poppie's and the Mucky Duck. Others, such as Auntie's and the Stab-in-the-Back, had forgotten their old names altogether.

'Working from the pub' was not considered unusual. In some newsrooms, so long as reporters wrote the name or phone number of their destination on the office black-board, they were free to follow their leads in the saloon bar. At the *Express*, one afternoon the editor came looking for his latest Hickey, and was told he was out for lunch. 'When did he go?' asked the editor. 'Last week,' came the reply. The management tolerated fraudulent expenses because its journalists were as addicted to the Street as to the sauce. This *modus vivendi* must have ruined many lives and livers but for the newspapers, in its grubby way, it worked.

A couple of miles west, *Private Eye* was a mixture of breakaway colony and rogue state, operating from a Soho that was scruffier and friendlier than today's. Though its once-drunken editor Richard Ingrams was now a teetotal churchgoer (and Dempster used to say, his 'hero') the pub was still central to its operation. In the Coach and Horses upstairs dining room, the *Eye* held its fortnightly lunches, where the central core of Old Salopians – Richard Ingrams, Christopher Booker, Willie Rushton and Paul Foot – were joined by Dempster, McKay and other trouble-makers. Evelyn Waugh's eldest son Auberon, the poet Christopher Logue and the racing correspondent Jeffrey Bernard all piled in, to swap stories and quiz more-or-less willing guests.

Grovel quickly became a mainstay of the *Eye*. Starting life as a monthly 'People' column, in March 1971 it acquired its proper name and logo – a top-hatted, monocled and bow-tied bounder, smoking through a cigarette holder – and a few months later, its signing-off 'Pip pip!'. Although most of its content was about other journalists' misdemeanours, it also cast aspersions about media darlings and, unlike the mainstream gossip columns, about the Royal Family. In the house style, they were called by silly soubriquets, the Queen being Glenda, her husband Phil the Greek and her sister Yvonne. And while Fleet Street generally maintained a discreet silence over the strutting Lord Snowdon, the *Eye* was delighted to report how 'Snowbum' had thrown wine over a toff who had displeased him at a dance, only for the drenched victim to turn and display his rear, saying: 'That's the only thing about me that could be of any interest to you.'

By now the *Eye* was recognisably the publication it is today, but this was its golden period. Under the aegis of the fictitious 'Lord Gnome', it offered the public ('Sid and Doris Bonkers') in the words of Auberon Waugh, 'an alternative perception of life in Britain which has had a profound effect on the nation's awareness of itself'. Inside the word-bubble cover, alongside the cartoons and lampoons, Grovel joined such regular features as True Stories – outlandish foreign news compiled by Logue – and Waugh's fantastical diary. Student Trotskyist 'Dave Spart', er, basically condemned the conspiracy of the military-industrial complex to enslave the working classes. Modern architecture was excoriated in Nooks and Corners (of the New Barbarism) and pretentious prose pilloried in Pseud's Corner. The word 'pseud' was actually a *Private Eye* invention that seeped into the popular usage; similarly, the name 'Grocer' for the Prime Minister Edward Heath.

In the same insidious way, Grovel's cast of characters permeated the public mind. One might need no opinion on Lady Antonia Fraser or the editor of the *Sunday Times*, but somehow it gladdened the heart to read of Lady

Magnesia Freelove's generosity with her affections or the fussy condescension of 'Dame' Harold Evans. Was it of any conceivable interest that Jocelyn 'Piranha Teeth' Stevens, now divested of *Queen* and a Fleet Street executive, was given to hurling filing cabinets out of windows? Was it of any moment that, in the *Eye*'s code for sex, a grand-child of Lord Beaverbrook hoped to 'discuss Uganda' with the feminist writer Germaine Greer? Enough for the *Eye* to maintain a circulation in the tens of thousands among a knowing elite.

What the reader could not know was the extent of Dempster's involvement. If he was not blaming McKay or his colleagues, he might deny working on Grovel altogether. The ambiguity was an insurance policy, like the squibs he wrote about himself. When Jon Bradshaw and Patrick Lichfield read in the *Eye* that 'Fleet Street's most notorious drunk, gambler, lecher and fortune hunter' was reconsidering his divorce since Emma de Bendern had come into another inheritance, they could hardly complain if they were called 'that backgammon bore and his pretty friend'.

Dempster once compared working on the *Eye* to riding a tiger. To be of his acquaintance must have felt much the same. And if he appeared snobbish and partial in his later years, he showed fewer signs of it in the Seventies. As Taki says: 'If a snob is someone who gives people respect because of their status, then he wasn't one at all. He only cared about someone grand when there was a story in them.' And Peter McKay adds that 'a fascination with the upper classes is a different pathology from a reverence for them'. Nor was he scared to bite the hand that fed him. When he moved to the *Mail* from the *Express*, you might have expected Grovel to show a little tact over the affairs of Dempster's ultimate paymaster, 'Mere' Vere Harmsworth, husband of the champagne-loving 'Bubbles' (another *Eye* name that stuck). No such luck.

The *Eye* even gloried in the humiliations that Harmsworth suffered through his association with Dempster. Noting that he had been blackballed by the Beefsteak, a gentleman's luncheon club, because of the diarist's dirt-digging, the magazine contrived to publish a letter sent on Harmsworth's behalf to the club's most senior member, the Duke of Devonshire. Written by Harmsworth's proposer – the Earl of Arran, an eccentric columnist on the now-defunct *Evening News* and a friend and employee of Harmsworth's father, the second Viscount Rothermere – it made hilarious reading:

> What do you think I should do – apart from leaving the country? Frankly the thought of telling Vere and of course Esmond [Rothermere] appalls me. As does the thought that I myself will have to resign, as I think your father did from the Turf when the late Lord Bearsted was pilled. I do not think the club would mind that much if I resigned, though it is now my only club, and I normally have luncheon there every day. Indeed, it would be like saying goodbye to a friend. Can I think that you might bring your considerable influence – I do not flatter you

– to bear on the situation?… This is a real *cri de coeur*.

Harmsworth was eventually admitted, leaving Dempster free to follow his contradictory calling. And if he had any qualms about his chosen path, he usually kept them to himself. Early in his career, he might grumble betimes that this was no job for a grown man; later, he might bemoan the fact that he could do nothing else. But the urge inside him to tell a story about someone, to spill the beans, always overrode his reservations. He was an insomniac, and claimed he spent the deep, still hours of the night plotting the downfall of his 'enemies'. But you do wonder. Did he think himself a doomed man, or a justified sinner?

In Haden-Guest's view, 'Nigel was very intelligent. He had a good analytical brain. But his love of gossip was secondary to his love of power – or at least the sense of power that he got from knowing other people's business. And they do say knowledge is power.' Another friend remembers a time they went to the cinema together and, chatting afterwards, 'Nigel showed no interest in the plot or the cinematography. All he talked about what how much the production cost, and who the producer was screwing. He had a rather dark view of life, and of people's motives. He didn't expect much of them – and he was seldom disappointed.'

Says Taki: 'He had some pat answers, about how you could judge public figures best by how they behaved in private – but then he'd be joking around again. He didn't want to talk about anything serious. My wife used to say he was always running away from himself, in case he didn't like what was there.' In a magazine profile of Dempster in his *Daily Mail* prime, Byron Rogers once wondered if, when he was alone, anyone at all was in the room.

POWER
'The Biggest Gossip in the World'

How the *Mail* became such a power in the land – and Dempster one of its sheriffs – has its roots in the lives of two press barons, and the death of a third. After Beaverbrook died in 1964, the *Express*' vigour and sales began their long slide – from four million to a current figure of about 700,000 a day. Exploiting this decline, Rupert Murdoch's yobbish *Sun* set new limits for what was lowbrow, but by treating cheap gossip as news, created a market of three to four million. And the following year, with the middle ground now redefined, Viscount Rothermere handed over the reins of his *Daily Sketch* and *Mail* to his son and heir.

Neither Vere Harmsworth's tabloid nor broadsheet title was in good health, both selling less than a million a day. But working with the *Sketch*'s editor, David English, Harmsworth devised a formula that would enrich them both and come to symbolise a very British state of mind. Subsuming the *Sketch*, on 3 May 1971 the *Mail* went 'compact'. (The nasty word 'tabloid' is never spoken there.) And though at first it was a thin thing of only 24 pages – and for many years, it lost money – the ploy paid off. By investing in a certain sort of talent, the *Mail*'s fortunes were so revived that even today, when the newspaper-buying habit is declining, it still has a daily circulation well above two million.

Its typography and design, its writers and subeditors, its appeal to middle-class women, its marketing, prejudices and politics – all these explain the rise of the *Mail* – but crucial to the mix would be an eponymous and fearless diarist, as an antidote to the unattributed Hickey. However, if Walter Winchell, the influential American columnist was the ideal, the *Mail* still had someway to go, settling instead for the fictional Suzy Knickerbocker from New York, on a vast fee of £1000 a week.

The heir to Cholly, Knickerbocker (real name Aileen Mehle) was a flop, a short lived-experiment, but she made the diary a talking point. English wanted her replacement to do the same – and if his first appointment had worked out, we might never have heard of Nigel Dempster. But Paul Callan was no match for his deputy, whohad crossed Fleet Street at English's invitation, arriving that November. 'He was a new type of person for the new type of paper that English was trying to create,' says the then junior reporter Rod Gilchrist, 'part of a culture shift away from the bully-boy, hard-drinking Scottish Mafia that ran Fleet Street.'

Dempster was at first known by fellow hacks as 'Lonely', after the snivelling grass in the Edward Woodward TV cop-show, *Callan*. But boasting that he could recite *Burke's Peerage*, 'Flash' knew too much of his milieu to believe the evidence of Callan's Old Etonian tie – and when he toppled him, would take vicious delight in revealing the state-school boy's imposture.

According to journalists' lore, he chose his moment when Callan was away in Blackpool, intending to write his column from the Labour Party Conference. Dempster produced from his bottom drawer a page's-worth of his own gossip – leading on the Aga Khan's instruction to his followers that they should leave strife-torn Uganda – and showed it to the editor. English, who was amused by 'creative tension', believing it led to better results, decreed that the diary should appear under Dempster's name for the next three days – during which time he also revealed that John Aspinall was to remarry and Henry Kissinger was considering retirement – and Callan's conference reports be reduced to a few paragraphs to run later in the week.

In fact, in Callan's absence, Dempster's name had been on the column before. (He had even attracted a libel writ from the publicity-averse Aga Khan, whose news Dempster delighted in spreading.) Also, it was Callan's bad luck that the *Mail*'s new political editor made his debut that week with lengthy dispatches from Blackpool. Still, back at the office, feeling slighted and snubbed, Callan insisted that English either move Dempster from his desk or accept his own resignation.

The editor bided his time. He sent Dempster for a few months to America – where his nickname was extended to 'Flashman' in the New York bureau – and unnerved Callan until the diarist wisely found a new berth. And if Dempster distinguished himself abroad by once crawling around on his hands and knees in Elaine's nightclub, pausing to bite the ankle of the socialite George Plimpton, English didn't mind. Who else could bring him an exclusive interview with Richard Burton – 'I can't live without her' – in which he bemoaned the collapse of his first marriage to Liz Taylor?

Dempster returned to Fleet Street in triumph, his first story – headlined 'The threesome: a happy event' – revealing that Lady Annabel Birley, estranged wife of the nightclub owner Mark Birley was expecting a child (now known as Jemima) by the tycoon James Goldsmith. This was news from the heart of Mayfair: Goldsmith was part of the 'Clermont Set' and a friend of Birley, who he first met at Eton. His crowd gathered round John Aspinall, at the casino he now ran in Berkeley Square. Birley ran Annabel's – named, ten years earlier, after his blushing bride – in the basement of the Clermont Club.

Although Goldsmith had been a target in the *Eye* before, never had Dempster snitched, on so grand a scale, under his own name – and there were various consequences.

Visiting Annabel's that night, Vere Harmsworth found himself barred (which only became known to his diarist some time later). Meanwhile, the feud between Dempster and Goldsmith that would last until the early Nineties was ratcheted up a notch. And Dempster became not only a *Daily Mail* star but a hate figure – damned if he dished, damned if he didn't.

One might find him tiresome – who cared that Princess Anne's husband Mark Phillips had visited a greasy spoon café, or that repairs to Prince Charles' Range Rover had cost £300? – but his access could not be denied. Besides, he still had the capacity to annoy. He revealed for example, that Lady Jacquetta Eliot was one of Lucian Freud's anonymous models; and (courtesy of his friend Taki) that a backgammon tournament on board the QE2 was hardly going swimmingly.

What's more, he had a talent to amuse. His chum Charles Benson was a purportedly hilarious character, in his time the 'bagman' for both Robert Sangster and the Aga Khan – and one of Dempster's greediest sources. Running a seaside picture of the Old Etonian racing tipster, he described him as 'a beached coelacanth'. Reporting on the original plans for the mosque in Regent's Park, he noted that they had the Saudi King Fahd's gift 'pointing towards Maidstone, not Mecca'.

Whilst it cannot be said that Dempster's writing had the brio and bluster of his conversation, even so, he had a flair for the pithy epithet, often combined with an insult, so that Harold Pinter was 'the socialist sourpuss',

the restaurateur Lord Forte 'the pint-sized peer' and Rod
Stewart 'the pixie-faced former gravedigger'. He could
be amusingly arch, too: 'Now we know what happened to
the curtains at Althorp, which [Lady Spencer] replaced.
She ran them up as an astonishing ball gown.' And if his
items sometimes seemed anodyne, that didn't mean they
were not having a more poisonous effect within a certain
social stratum. As he said to one colleague: 'It's not what
you print but what you don't print that matters. You have
to word it so that they know you know the unprintable
truth.'

But one of the virtues of the diary was its comforting sameness. With his assistants, Dempster developed
a distinctive, slightly long-winded style that enabled
him to fill a page every day. There were several key
features. The British obsession with property prices
was accommodated wherever possible – 'her £200,000
Chelsea town house', 'his £1 million Scottish estate'. An
omniscient 'I' was very much in evidence: – 'news reaches me', 'I hear that' – and readers were reminded of any
romantic or family history. Even when his subjects had
regular parts in his malign comedy, these little sketches
would be repeated *ad infinitum*.

Something of a comedy villain, like Piers Morgan or
Simon Cowell today, Dempster was an easy target –
literally in 1974, when Patrick Lichfield locked him in
the stocks at a charity do and then 'lost' the key, so that the
diarist was pelted with rotten eggs all night. (He gamely
returned the next year to play the butler in a *What the*

Butler Saw tableau.) The writer Clive James once said that his revelations of infidelities sent children crying home from school – a charge that Dempster denied, though the Duchess of York confirms she first learned of her parents' 1974 divorce through his column. But whatever distaste the public affected for the messenger, an increasing number of them couldn't get enough of his message.

He was trouncing his competitors. So when, in 1975, he gave the inside track on the actress Vivien Merchant's divorce from playwright Harold Pinter – in which Lady Antonia Fraser was cited as correspondent – it was unsurprising that he attracted the odium of the broadsheets (who could then repeat the juicy facts at one remove). Paul Slickey was disinterred. It was noted that the permissive society had not made such news more boring to read, but easier to write. Scarfe illustrated a worthy *Sunday Times* piece with cartoon of a fly on a dung heap.

And why this synthetic fury? Dempster had already drawn attention to the Pinter-Fraser friendship before in both the *Mail* and the *Eye*, much to the embarrassment of Lady Antonia's husband Sir Hugh Fraser MP. Merchant had announced: 'I am specifically naming Antonia because if she wants to play silly games with my husband, I am prepared to do the same to her.' But the day after this, Dempster named the phalanx of other admirers* that the

---

*Alas, it is untrue – as first reported by *Private Eye* in April 1974 - that Lady Antonia dismissed Clive James' suit with the immortal put-down 'I only sleep with the First Eleven'…

aristocratic authoress had collected – and to which he had been alerted – during her 19 years of marriage.

Under the headline 'The Romantic Life Style of Lady Antonia Fraser', he printed the smiling pictures and details of five men: the actor Robert Stephens, ex-husband of Maggie Smith; Jonathan Aitken, one of the famous family, recently elected Tory MP for Thanet and not yet a perjurer; ex-King Constantine of Greece; Rupert Lycett Green, the husband of John Betjeman's daughter Candida; and Lord Lambton, then two years into his retirement from government after a prostitution scandal. In the body of the text, two more men were named: the banker Jacob Rothschild, and the Duke of Beaufort's heir Lord (David) Somerset.

On the trail of his scoop, Dempster was like a man possessed. Almost a year before, he had written in the *Eye* that Robert Stephens was 'opening the batting this season' with Lady Antonia (and that she had threatened 'a newspaper' with a £100,000 libel suit if it printed the story in less euphemistic form). The night before his story ran, 'he practically dragged Robert Stephens off the stage', according to a colleague. And Stephens unwisely confirmed that he and she had had a 'light hearted' romance the year before. 'Antonia and I were very much in love, but things started to get a bit difficult,' he said, after she met Pinter at a party from which both their spouses had left early.

For several months, Dempster would return to the adulterous couple, charting their domestic arrangements

at the discreet little house in Kensington to which Pinter
had moved. The day after the 'outing', however, he
produced a comic sequel. Having cajoled Merchant out of
self-imposed purdah, he quoted her verdict on Pinter's flit:
'He didn't need to take a change of shoes. He can always
wear Antonia's. She has very big feet, you know.' Elated
by his own devilry, Dempster accompanied this paragraph
with pictures of the feet in question, and included Sir
Hugh's for good measure.

***

Dempster now claimed that he prevented more
adultery than the Archbishop of Canterbury. So when
challenged about the propriety of such intrusion, he told
one journalist that he felt justified after he saw Pinter
and Fraser necking in the theatre stalls in front of him.
Meanwhile, the *Observer*'s Michael Davie hinted that
Dempster might emulate Lord Balcairn – the diarist in
Evelyn Waugh's *Vile Bodies* – and put his head in an oven.
And there were the routine cries for privacy laws. But
Waugh's son Auberon sprung to the defence of his *Private
Eye* colleague in the *New Statesman*. There was a principle
at stake, he argued:

> 'It is one of the oldest pastimes of the poor and unprivi-
> leged to gossip about the rich and powerful... [and] I
> would have thought it a small price to pay for being rich,
> or beautiful, or exceptionally talented, or even famous.

If, as a famous person, you are in the habit of doing things which would make you ashamed if they were more widely known then you have a clear choice between changing your habits, changing your attitude to them or retreating from the public stage. The other course of action is to cross your fingers and hope Nigel Dempster never finds out, but I do not think it reasonable to expect the entire structure of a free press to be dismantled in order to accommodate your foibles.'

Actually, much that Dempster 'found out' was inaccurate, if not defamatory. To the extent that it influenced public opinion, his revelation that Denis Thatcher had been married before was genuine news. But over a fortnight, he announced the forthcoming marriages of Jerry Hall and Bryan Ferry, Davina Sheffield and Prince Charles, and Nancy Andrews and Ringo Starr – all wrongly. Still, Waugh's point was proved at the end of 1975, when Dempster predicted the Prime Minister's resignation a full three months before Harold Wilson's declining powers made it inevitable. The story came from the political reporter Gordon Greig, via David English. An informant had overheard a remark made by Foreign Secretary James Callaghan, and Dempster brazened out a writ to prove Greig was right. 'Writs,' he said – and was forever quoted as saying – 'are the Oscars of my profession.'

The tribute he was given, however, was a television documentary on BBC2, when this was the thinking person's channel. And though it had its moments – the bad old dowager Margaret, Duchess of Argyll declaring that, while journalists wore two hats in the Thirties, they now wore none at all – this was not Dempster's finest hour. The *Sunday Times* critic called it the 'portrait of an oddly obsessive character, whose combination of worldly ambition and dedicated malice might have been invented by Balzac' – and for good measure called him 'hypocritically defensive... fatuously conceited... naively snobbish... chillingly puritanical... and committed to disloyalty'.

It was not how he was seen in the office. Gilchrist remembers him as 'a really popular figure, particularly with us "underclass". He was our star, always ready to take on the big guys. We loved the way he played by different rules. We thought, "If he can have that life, maybe we can, too." And in those days – when the *Mail* was still losing money – he gave us much-needed inspiration and confidence.' Liz Brewer echoes the praise. After he libelled her, she wrote to complain, but earned his undying gratitude by renouncing legal action. Thereafter, 'he was always happy to give a mention to any event or establishment that I was promoting if he thought it deserved it'.

It was no wonder Dempster was warned off applying to join the intelligentsia's Garrick Club. But that wasn't enough to deter him from his mission to amuse the middle classes with the pratfalls of the privileged. Even in these enlightened times, the story of Maureen Colquhoun would probably raise a smile – but in December 1976, it caused amazement. Dempster disclosed that the Labour MP for

Northampton North had left her husband for Babs Todd, former director of the lesbian magazine *Sappho* – and announced it with a housewarming invitation that depicted two women embracing. Her local party subsequently deselected her, citing a remark of hers about the need to take Enoch Powell's racial views seriously – and a punch she had landed on the nose of a car park attendant.

At *Private Eye*, Dempster was dubbed ' the 'Greatest Living Englishman', a complicated pun that honoured his *lèse majesté*, acknowledged the editor behind him and affectionately mocked his background. But by then, the magazine was locked in a legal battle with the newly knighted James Goldsmith – over its allegations about his involvement in the legendary Lucan Affair – and Dempster played an uncomfortable part in the drama.

Another member of the macho Clermont Set, Lord Lucan became infamous in 1974, when he bungled the murder of his wife – killing their nanny instead – and fled London, never to be found. While Lady Lucan went to hospital to recover, one of the unhappy couple's friends, the artist and socialite Dominic Elwes, talked to the *Sunday Times'* James Fox and revealed there had been a lunch for the Set, when the protection of Lucan had been discussed (while Elwes had been dispatched to visit his traumatised wife). Elwes also introduced Fox to John Aspinall, who praised the killer's 'old fashioned qualities', said that anyone in the same situation would have attempted the same crime, and agreed that if Lucan had asked him for help, he would have given it.

When the article came out, it was illustrated by one of Elwes' portraits – a group shot of the Set, including the painter, Goldsmith, Aspinall and Lucan – and was deeply hostile to 'these weird and thoroughly unpleasant people'. For his fee, Elwes received £200. For his troubles, he was barred from the Clermont by John Aspinall and from Annabel's by Mark Birley. Some years earlier, he had been celebrated for eloping to Cuba with the heiress Tessa Kennedy. But now in his early forties, divorced and a manic-depressive, he depended on his clan. Cast out, he committed suicide in the autumn of 1975, leaving a note that read: 'I curse Mark and Jimmy from beyond the grave. I hope they are happy now.'

Enter *Private Eye* – and Dempster, who among others supplied information for an article in which Goldsmith was put at the centre of this sorry business. Wrongly, as it turns out, he was accused of obstructing police enquiries, chairing the post-murder lunch (as first reported in the *Sunday Times*), excluding Elwes from it and discussing plans to assist Lucan. Associates at Slater Walker, his recently acquired investment bank, were dragged in, too, and questions were raised over his fitness to 'guide the helm of a great public enterprise'.

After further attacks on his business dealings, in January 1976 Goldsmith issued 63 writs against the magazine and 30 of its distributors. He also applied to the High Court to bring proceedings for criminal libel over the lunch allegations, disclosing that he hadn't even been a guest. Nearly two years of litigation followed, and several other excellent books cover this ground. In brief, after *Private Eye*'s extraordinary fund-raising campaign – which included a leotard-clad Dempster grappling with the wrestler Johnny Kwango in front of 10,000 spectators at Stamford Bridge – the result for Goldsmith was vindication; for the *Eye* a huge surge in popularity; and for the diarist more notoriety.

He revelled in it – 'There is a holiday in my heart when I discover another marriage break up' was one of his lines – and seemed determined to prove that he was a very wicked man, who could still perform better drunk than his rivals could sober. Friends now make his existence sound like one long lunch. He took regular tables at San Lorenzo, the Savoy, Langan's and Drones (the latter run by the wealthy Nicky Kerman, who was as central to the scene as Dempster and host of a regular Sunday dinner). 'It was,' says Antony Rufus-Isaacs, 'open house. You simply rang Dempster, asked where lunch was and turned up. There would be 20 people at a time, all paid for by the *Daily Mail*.'

The lunches he held on Friday – his day off – were particularly riotous affairs and carried on for 25 years. If he wasn't joining Richard Ingrams at the Gay Hussar, Dempster and his muckers from the deb decade and the Chelsea Set would meet at a restaurant in their old stamping-ground: Leonardo's, Monkey's, Dan's – and often latterly at Foxtrot Oscar in Royal Hospital Road – to trade jovial insults and top each other's tall tales.

And drink. Dempster always broke up the day with

a bottle of chilled Chablis – sometimes two – unless he was needed in the office. Then he would pop across to El Vino's for a couple of bottles of champagne. Cracking jokes, sometimes throwing punches, he was the epitome of a Fleet Street character (and the source of some £30,000 in tip fees a year). Back at the *Mail*, he kept an oxygen tank and mask behind his desk, so that he and his team of three could take a blast and clear their heads.

Although there is general agreement that Dempster 'had hollow legs', one does wonder if he had a self-destructive streak? A need to see how far he could push things, as he had at Sherborne – or just the boozer's urge to obliterate any self-knowledge? In a 'day in the life' feature for *Women's Own* magazine he gave an interview that was by turns bombastic, beguiling and plain bonkers. Under the headline 'I'm the Biggest Gossip in the World', he commented: 'There has been talk that my world is one which I've trumped up for myself. It's been described as a limbo through which a succession of apparently doomed figures float: bankers, gamblers, tax-evaders, lechers. Nonsense. I am the prophet of my time – but no one will listen.'

Dempster revealed that he relied on his memory rather than take notes, 'which put people off'. Estimating his average alcoholic intake at four bottles a day, he said he hardly ate at lunchtime but ensured that the drink flowed because 'it helps people lose their inhibitions', and described a routine that might sound exhausting and pointless to some but not unenviable to others. Starting with his legendary jog, he stopped *en route* to the office for a swim or game of squash at the Royal Automobile Club, put in a couple of hours' work either side of lunch and – punctuating it with calls to his New York and Hollywood stringers – ended his day with a trawl of Morton's 'to find the likes of Terence Stamp', followed by Tramp and Maunkberry's, the Clermont and Crockford's.

'If the hallmarks of my column are money, sex and innuendo, that's because it's what people want to read about,' said Dempster. 'As to offending people, whom do I offend? Only the upper classes. They're only one per cent of the population; 90 per cent adore me.'

***

Dempster might not have been every girl's idea of a dream husband—but he had something that in 1977 convinced a well-known heiress that he was the man for her. She was, however, the very opposite of what the words 'well-known heiress' connote. Lady Camilla Dorothy Godolphin Harris, (née Osborne), nine years Dempster's junior, was as much remarked on for her misfortune as her fortune, a very private individual who had no great interest in the popular press and no small desire to stay out of it.

Her father was the bibulous 11th Duke of Leeds who – as Dempster never tired of repeating – was the brother-in-law of the late Queen Mother. A tax exile with homes in Jersey and the South of France, he died when his daughter was 12. A man Camilla once described as looking like 'a very grand wine waiter', his idea of heaven would have been drinking Martinis in a cinema. Oblivious to his title, and uninterested in living up to it, he was supposedly a socialist, a cause he certainly supported in the redistribution of his own wealth. Rattling around in Melbourne House, his white-faced square Victorian mansion, if not as uxorious as Lord Kimberley, he still had to pay out for one breach of promise, and may have married his third and last duchess rather than do the same again.

'He was quite like Nigel in his self-centredness,' says Camilla. The daughter of the Duke's second wife, she was left behind when her mother bolted. An only and lonely child, it is said she would knock on neighbours' doors and ask if there was anyone she could play with – and her sense of solitude must have been heightened when the wranglings between the Dukes's second and third wives on his death led to her being made a ward of court in 1963. In that state, she went to boarding school in the West Country, then Queens Gate in London, and divided the rest of her time between the 2nd Duchess (remarried and now called Lady Lawrence) and her father's third wife.

Both her trust fund allowance and the £1 million she would inherit at 21 meant that Camilla attracted the attention of journalists and suitors. She appeared in magazines' 'most eligible' lists, and replied to their questions politely. During her deb year, she stayed with her uncle, Lord Chandos, who would repel bounty hunters by pretending to be the butler when he answered the phone and asking if he could take a message. 'Commie Camilla' as she was known, read the *Guardian* and agreed with its editorials. But wherever she went, she never quite blended in. A year after entering Newcastle University to read Philosophy and English, she left – 'No one understood my accent' – and a year after that, she had bought a house in Markham Square, Chelsea, and become engaged to advertising man Robert Harris.

Divorce proceedings began in 1973. 'We are not compatible,' said Camilla, who was left with a ten-month old daughter, Emily. For a couple of years, she went to ground, moving to a flat in Cadogan Gardens and burying herself in books, but by 1975, it was announced – in Dempster's column, no less – that she 'was planning wedding number two', to the PR Christopher Moorsom. Unfortunately for the diarist's reputation if not his future happiness, Camilla got cold feet – leaving her available when the pair met through one of her old school friends.

In Erika Dempster's recollection, 'Nigel didn't do the asking. She was determined to have him. He said: "There's this girl Camilla who wants to marry me, and I don't know what to do."' Perhaps he was tickled that James Goldsmith's father had been best friends with the 11th Duke, but as Camilla remembers it, 'He said he was rescuing me from a very middle aged life. I think he saw me as a challenge. Enough people told me he was trouble...' Knowing her interest in French cuisine, he booked their first dinner at Le Français on the Fulham Road, before – 'talk about drunk' – going on to Tramp.

The man with no background and the woman who didn't want one had found their match. They married at Chelsea Registry Office in July 1977, to the perplexity of Camilla's mother and stepmother. No family from either side was invited, but the small wedding was enlivened on the town hall steps by the assorted hacks who came to make affectionate mockery. With what intent or sincerity it's impossible to gauge, Dempster told one: 'I hope the *Mail*'s got some other job for me. I've only seen the editor on two occasions recently. You can only do it for so long.'

It was also reported that in the evening the Dempsters would be going to Peter Cadbury's dance in the country, then staying with Lord Beaverbrook's grandson Johnny Kidd; and it was noted that, while the couple arranged a family house, they would be living separately. Soon, however, he and Camilla were settled off the Fulham Road, in four floors of Neville Terrace, with decoration by Christophe Gollut and fine paintings on the walls. They had their daughter Louisa in 1979, and when Camilla came into another chunk of family money in 1987, bought a second house for weekends. A spacious and pretty lodge overlooking Ham Common – where she still lives – it was convenient for the Kempton Park races and as near the countryside as either could bear.

The marriage was much happier at the beginning than the end. Between his job and the racecourse, Dempster was out of the house a great deal, and in it 'a little of him went a long way,' says Camilla. 'He was very overpowering.' She would accompany him to social functions 'when they sounded like fun to me' (which they seldom did) but steered clear of his 'boy's club'. To her, his intimates seemed very immature – and 'no doubt they saw me as a killjoy and a nag'.

Possibly an obstruction, too. Camilla says she has no knowledge of her husband's infidelity ('and if I had found out, I'm sure he would have been able to convince me otherwise') but as Taki puts it, 'Nigel was always chasing pussy'. One can only guess at his motives, and his fear of discovery. Peter McKay has said his old colleague would 'stab *himself* in the back for the sake of a good story' – but why would he risk career-suicide, to the rejoicing of his critics and rivals?

In interviews the self-appointed moral arbiter would even volunteer that he was 'not an adulterer', adding that if he were, he would be fair game. But Taki is insistent. In his high-rolling circle, Dempster's dalliance with a Middle Eastern *grande dame* is considered common knowledge – 'He would talk about her himself,' they say – and if he was more circumspect about the authoress Tessa Dahl, 16 years his junior, it was quite common knowledge at the *Mail* that they slept together before and during his second marriage.

'Nigel wasn't driven by sex so much as people,' says Dahl. 'And though I know other women who say he wasn't so good in bed, I thought he was a great lover.' Above all, though, he was her friend. Since first meeting over the gaming tables at the Curzon Club – where the

15-year-old Dahl had been smuggled in by her father Roald – she 'adored him', she says, 'and he seldom let me down'. She recalls on that first occasion in 1972 that 'a friend of my father's told me Nigel had been paid off by some girl's father to stay away from her – so naturally I was fascinated'. Seeing him at a premiere three years later, she reintroduced herself, and soon became both his regular escort and a character in his column.

'I was unknown before Nigel started writing about me,' she says. 'Then he contributed the text about me to Lichfield's book, *The 100 Most Beautiful Women in the World*, and a very nice feature in *Woman* magazine. I was very flattered, of course, and we became mates – not dates, we didn't start with sex – and went to parties together. We both came from mongrel backgrounds and had the same view of people, the same jaded eye. I was very observant, although I wasn't yet writing, and he liked my observations. In fact, I often had to ring him the next morning to remind him what had happened as he'd been too drunk to remember.'

Dahl was married from 1981 to 1986 – 'I'll give it six months,' Dempster told her at the reception – and again in 1991. Before and between those times, if with decreasing frequency, she would sleep with him – 'at his house when Camilla was away' – and though she was supposed to be a good friend of her lover's wife, 'that was only by accident, because of my relationship with Nigel, so I'm afraid I never felt guilty about it'.

Citing all Dempster's usual attractions – his charm,

kindness and humour, the joy in anarchy that he shared with her father – she adds to them 'his complications. And I like a complicated man.' To her he seemed 'almost manic depressive – and perhaps the drink was self-medication'. One minute, 'he'd be proclaiming world domination', the next 'saying he'd screwed up his career'. But, she says, 'he had no delusions about himself. He knew he was a snob, he knew he could be impossible. He knew he wanted to be on an equal footing with his friends but wasn't really on the inside – and he knew he didn't really respect them. Those contradictions were the undercurrent of his life.'

She remembers going with Dempster to one of William Piggott-Brown's dinners, 'when that crowd were at the height of their aristocratic arrogance', and suffering an evening of schoolboy sexual humour: 'Nigel joined in, but when we got back to the car, we just sat there in amazement for about an hour. He thought they were a bunch of fucking prats.' As for his marriage, she's unwilling to take sides. One night, Camilla came to stay with Dahl when she walked out on Dempster. Another time, she saw him 'absolutely devastated' when he discovered Camilla was seeing someone else.

Before Camilla, says Dahl, 'there were plenty of women throwing themselves at Nigel's feet'. Likewise there were those with whom he was 'obsessed', among them the model Carol Edge, and the 'glamour' girl Erica Creer. But according to Ingrid Seward – then a PR for the British arm of the *Playboy* organisation, later a journalist on the royal beat and wife of the writer Ross Benson – 'Nigel didn't really go out with anyone. He had regular girlfriends, and slept with them, but the sex didn't seem to mean anything to him. In fact, I'm not sure he liked women that much.' Many of his contemporaries, perhaps confusing his campness with other proclivities, wonder if there was a gay streak to Nigel. Anna Wintour simply says: 'That's English men for you.'

So when Dempster announced his engagement to the retiring daughter of the duke, knowing looks were exchanged among his friends. 'People thought Nigel was marrying her for the security and status,' says Dahl, 'but he did love her, too, even if he was a bit frightened of her.' And however much he liked the expensive Chinese vases and family furniture, or the duke's old coronets displayed in a glass case in the dining room, they were secondary to his respect for Camilla. 'He admired her no-nonsense approach,' says Dahl. 'Still, he could be very naughty and not the most loyal in his telling tales about the women both in and out of his life.'

Among them, according to one *Mail* colleague, were at least 'two half-hearted affairs' during his second marriage. But this source agrees that 'Nigel wasn't particularly motivated by sex. I know a *madame* who offered him all sorts of girls, and he just didn't want to know.' As for Dahl, after her father's death in 1990, Tessa – who was already a case study in psychiatric illness – became addicted to alcohol and cocaine in what the American magazine *People* called a 'drink and drugs spiral'. Asked to make a comment in the piece by its reporter, Dempster said his old bedmate was 'in terminal decline' — and that, Dahl says, made her 'absolutely furious'. But they made up in the end, 'and he was very supportive and involved in my recovery'.

104

GLORY
The Toast of the Turf

The second Mrs Dempster thinks Dahl's stories should
be taken with a pinch of salt. At first she and her
errant spouse were happy enough – although she preferred him in January, when he went on the wagon. ('He
wanted to prove to himself that he wasn't an alcoholic,' says
Camilla.) Still, he captivated her. He told her his favourite
book was *The Great Gatsby* – and one wonders if he abhorred
the 'vast carelessness' of the rich. He had in common with
her a real passion for the ballet, and lied that he had a box
at Covent Garden: 'But he said things just because he liked
the sound of them.' They also shared the experience of
an older, distant father – and 'in different ways, a boredom with the Establishment'. More importantly, he made

her laugh. She recounts how, when she was pregnant, they went to a drinks party where Princess Margarret was one of the guests. Finding the lift temporarily out of order, he dragged Camilla up several flights of stairs – and when the squiffy princess began to commiserate with his expectant wife, cut in, 'But that's social climbing, ma'am.'

Not that he was always so polished. In 1978, he was reprimanded by the Racing Information Bureau for his behaviour in June at Epsom's Playboy Derby. The prelude was a 'hair-raising' drive with Ingrid Seward. ('We were going on the central reservation, the hard shoulder, the grass verge – he wouldn't be held up.') But it all kicked off in the press room, after Christopher Wilson, from the Hickey column, playfully locked his rival's assistant into the *Mail's* telephone box. When the news was carried to Dempster in the stands, he returned to the press room, collared Wilson and socked him on the chin. A mêleé followed and top hats flew, while the *Telegraph's* correspondent Lord Oaksey – standing on a table to take the money – offered 6 to 4 to win on Dempster and evens on Wilson.

After wrestling on the floor for a while, Wilson invited his adversary to 'take it outside'. Unsatisfied, Wilson ripped out the *Mail's* press room phone line – and was last seen that day running from the course with Dempster in pursuit. Later that month, there was a rematch at Ascot. The Dempster team arrived with pots of thick hair cream, cornered the Hickey mob and plastered them with it. More punches were thrown, soda siphons were squirted and another reporter was locked in a phone booth.

It was this sort of behaviour that actually endeared him to Tina Brown, now a mighty power in the media, then a young hack making a name for herself at the *Evening Standard* and *Sunday Telegraph* magazine. 'He was a force for anarchy,' she says, 'and I loved him for it.' Brown met Dempster through Auberon Waugh, who she had originally interviewed for *Isis*, the Oxford University journal. After graduating and finding work in Fleet Street, she became a semi-detached member of the *Private Eye* crew. 'And as I was always being assigned high-society pieces, we often encountered each other at the same events.'

A 'devoted fan' of Dempster's column, 'which was an art form that nobody has ever matched', Brown found his writing 'hysterically funny, the way he could capture some-one in a phrase', and was no less impressed by his tall tales in conversation. 'I guess I hero-worshipped him,' she says. 'He represented a London in which I hadn't yet arrived.' And Dempster returned the respect. Although 'he liked hanging out with young girls' – on one occasion taking her and Tessa Dahl on another 'terrifying' drive to the Derby – when she had a 'little romance' with his friend Garth Wood, 'Nigel was very disapproving, like a clucking mentor'.

Dempster could clearly spot talent. Having briefly been a covert contributor to *Tatler**, in the summer of 1979 he was offered the editorship of the magazine by its new owner – the Australian millionaire Gary Bogard – but

* When *Tatler* was owned by the scapegrace Johnny Elliott, Dempster was engaged to write a column called 'Tittle Tattle' with Liz Brewer in 1977 – but after allowing a libel to appear, he made his excuses and left.

turned it down, recommending young Brown instead. She in turn tried to 'break him out as a writer' while at the helm of the magazine, but eventually decided he was 'a quintessential miniaturist – he couldn't keep it up for more than about six paragraphs.' However, she says, 'he was both an inspiration, in his impish mercilessness, and a great help.' When she needed a telephone number or an idea, she only had to call him. But when she needed background, he could be less obliging: 'You'd call him about an idea you'd had, and open the *Mail* the next day to see he'd written your story.' There was, she admits a 'dangerous, ruthless' side to Dempster – 'he was given to flights of venom, one didn't know quite why' – and after *Private Eye* began to attack her husband Harry Evans, she decided to keep an amicable distance, seeing him 'every five years or so'.

Meanwhile, Dempster was repelling attacks himself. In December 1979 he had to face down the combined might of Sir James Goldsmith and Vere Harmsworth (who had now inherited his late father's title of Lord Rothermere and relocated to Paris as a tax exile). Sore from his own battles with *Private Eye*, Goldsmith wrote to the *Mail*'s proprietor, pointing out that Dempster was part of the *Eye's* 'inner circle' and 'a proven liar', before asking whether it was 'compatible with a healthy press that [he] should be a senior journalist on a respected national newspaper'. Looking to his circulation, Rothermere found a different pretext for attack. In a memo to Dempster, he observed:

Your column in the last few months has, in my view, deteriorated and I commented to the Editor that it had been showing all [the] signs of neglect, had become boring and most people were preferring to read Hickey which had become lively and amusing. You were devoting far too much space to foreigners of no particular interest to our readership and a tired roster of well known names which had been going round the London Gossip Columns for years and years such as David Frost, Sir Charles Clore and many others. Your column one might say was beginning to have the taste of an old cold fried potato.

Apparently hurt, certainly fearless, Dempster came out fighting. Taking a long-owed holiday, he told the trade press he had defended himself in a reply to Rothermere, and was also supported by David English: 'This week I saw my editor, who told me he had been asked to sack me. But he refused to do so for three reasons. He told me that I was an asset to his newspaper; that in the light of Sir James' letter it would make Lord Rothermere look silly; and that my firing would cause untold trouble with my *Mail* colleagues and the unions.'

This was true – newspapers in the Seventies only appeared by courtesy of corrupt and prickly trades unions – and Dempster now played them to perfection. Attending a chapel meeting, he stood on a chair and gave a rousing speech, saying that his problem today would be theirs tomorrow – 'It was like Henry V at Agincourt,' says Rod

Gilchrist – and received a rousing cheer. Still, he was also unbelievably cheeky, not only castigating his proprietor in public but going on to cast aspersions ón Rothermere's tax status: 'It is just extraordinary that the only one who criticises my column lives abroad.'

There was more. Dempster complained that his rival on Hickey had twice as many staff, worked a four- instead of five-day week and earned £6000 more than his basic salary of £12,000. Noting that his column was a 'highlight of the paper' and had been used in advertisements, he continued: 'I can't see how I can continue working at the *Mail* with these extraordinary allegations hanging over me.' Yet he did. Though Grovel named Rothermere 'Shit of the Year' in 1980, within twelve months, supported behind the scenes by the proprietor's colourful wife, Dempster had trebled his pre-bonus salary, reduced his hours from 46 to 32 weeks a year and been given a 'picture byline'. Grinning toothily, balding faster than his official photographs showed, he now presided over what was probably the best-read page in Fleet Street, a pleasure – guilty or otherwise – enjoyed by millions five days a week.

'He was quite simply the best known journalist in Britain, possibly the world,' says his eventual successor at the *Mail*, Richard Kay. He was what we now call a celebrity. And when his old rival Ross Benson later labelled him 'a self-made man who has come to worship his own creator', he had a point. Dempster treated his life as if it were a play in which he was the principal.

As Ed Victor, later his agent, comments: 'He took

on a part, and he played it to perfection – the way he dressed immaculately, everything.' Even behind the row with Rotheremere, one can detect a sort of theatre. For a year before his memo, 'Mere' Vere had been a regular target in *Private Eye*. Grovel first revealed his plans for tax avoidance, and his bedroom arrangements with the 'octoroon hand model' Maiko Lee. To some extent, the backer and his star turned their spat into a show.

At this distance of time, and given the state of our media now, the buzz there used to be around Dempster may seem bizarre. But he and his editor had a deep and innate understanding of the middle-British mindset in the latter part of the 20th century. As many pundits have noted, the *Mail* both 'cut across and reinforced' the class system. In so doing, it responded to its readers, who were motivated as much by envy as aspiration. Acacia Avenue needed confirmation from Dempster that 'they' were no better than 'us', before following 'their' lead.

It wasn't often that Dempster got to publish a scandal about a Goldsmith or Pinter under his own name. Most of his stories came from the new B-List, so brilliantly described by Tina Brown in her book, *Life as a Party*: 'Resting model girls with Uvasun tans, gay crimpers in lift-and-separate trousers, pancaked promotions stylists, tinted interior designers, pidgin-English shoe designers, disc-jockeys on the pull, fashion editors on the twirl, film stars on the wane, debutantes on the game, *bon viveurs* on the dole, peers of the realm on parole, all having a ball. They are no longer classified as fashionable bits of colour, as they were in the Sixties, reassuringly outnumbered by the Real Thing. They have taken over, big-banged, formed their own galaxy. In the face of their exploding heat, aristocratic society shrinks inwards or goes up for sale.'

So Dempster found himself reporting the latest party thrown by *Playboy* Europe boss Victor Lownes at Wedgie's (formerly Club del Aretusa). He filled his column with the staffing difficulties of the new Countess Spencer, and the propensity of Sir William Piggott-Brown to 'streak' naked through parties or of his friend Dai Llewellyn to propose to wealthy young women. He had friends in high places, too: at Nicholas Haslm's *tenue de chasse* party at his Hampshire country house – a wall-to-wall aristocratic affair – Brown reports Dempster springing 'from table to table like a Demon Prince shouting "Sauciness! Sauciness! I must find sauciness. I know it's somewhere in this tent!"' But if one wonders why he dwelled so much on some rather dubious characters, the true answer is that a large swathe of Society's old guard had become rather wary of him.

Michael Corry-Reid, who became a friend in the early Eighties, remembers inviting Dempster to his house in Chelsea for a Christmas drinks party which several well-known people were also attending, 'And Nigel seemed genuinely surprised. He said: "Me? You're inviting me to a private party?" I said: "So long as you don't write about it."' And he was as good as gold.' Nonetheless, there was a sad postscript to the occasion. 'I later received a long letter from one guest, who was really furious that I could have invited Nigel. He said, "How dare you let that scum into the house when I was there?" I kept it to myself, but a while later, this person's name came up in conversation and Nigel said, "Oh, he's one of my biggest sources." I didn't have the heart to tell him about the letter.'

In his column, though, Dempster achieved the desired effect. Battered by his liberal use of the first person pronoun, his followers believed the diarist was a part of the world on which he reported so much better than his so-called rivals. He had his catch lines, 'You read it here first' and 'Watch this space', and his daily 'PS' item in the 'basement' of the page. He was even worth gossiping about himself – and only too ready to oblige. A pilot for his own TV chat show was naturally plugged. ('He desperately wanted that to succeed and was always frustrated that he didn't come across well on television,' says Tessa Dahl.) But even if his house was burgled or his car scratched, his wallet stolen or his luggage lost, Dempster would let his readers know. And actually, his own escapades were no less exciting than those of his subjects. It just depended on their propriety whether he or his competitors relayed them. After announcing in 1980 that he would enter the first London Marathon, he treated the world to regular training reports (and ran several more). After he was arrested for drink driving, others did the honours.

There was something about this incident that typified the man. Pulled over for speeding on Kennington Road, he was deemed to be smelling of alcohol and asked to take a breathalyser test – but strangely for such an athlete, found himself unable sufficiently to inflate the bag. Taken to the local police station for a blood test, he claimed a phobia of needles but said he was willing to have a sample taken from his big toe. In the words of the court reporter, this was 'technically impossible and the police took the offer as a refusal' – an offence for which he was duly charged. However, before the formalities were completed, he said he would give a urine specimen, only to be told it was too late for the procedure to be effective. Dempster had slipped through a loophole. His solicitor pointed out that it was legally incumbent on the police to offer such a test. Dempster claimed that he had not been drinking and any odour was due to a 'special diet'. The case was dismissed.

***

In the same circumstances, a lesser being might have been given his marching orders, but Dempster was now so important to the *Mail* that he was almost untouchable. Few in Fleet Street were as well placed to report on the impending marriage of Prince Charles and Lady Diana Spencer, which he announced in September 1980. (To some extent, this compensated for the false predictions he had recently made of Prince Charles's engagements to Princess Marie-Astrid of Luxembourg, Lady Jane Wellesley and Miss Anna Wallace.) As David English knew, when Prince Charles was supposedly wooing Diana, Dempster had referred in *Private Eye*'s Grovel column to his simultaeneous assignations with Camilla Parker-Bowles (whose best friend had the bad luck to be married to the diarist's informant Charles Benson).

Moreover, he knew where the bodies were buried in the momentous case of Princess Margaret, her ex-husband Lord Snowdon and her toy boy lover Roddy Llewellyn, brother of 'Dirty Dai' and now gardener by canny appointment to Dempster himself. This royal knock-about was probably Britain's biggest gossip story of the Seventies, and Dempster had a ringside seat.

The diarist amused the princess the first time he met her, in 1971. He told her how he'd got the scoop on a bishop and his mistress after seeing a 40D-cup brassiere on the episcopal washing line. He also proved himself a trusty: while *Private Eye*'s Grovel spared her no blushes, in the *Mail*, Dempster stuck to the Fleet Street line of knowing innuendo. And if they were hostages to each other, then each also suffered Stockholm Syndrome. In 1981 – a decade before the journalist Andrew Morton became the mouth-piece for Princess Diana – their odd alliance bore fruit in a biography. Started two years earlier, *Princess Margaret, A Life Unfulfilled* (on which the following account largely relies) was probably Dempster's best work. For all his reverence for its subject, he drew a fascinating and informed picture of her world, reflecting the wider world in it.

Curiosity had been growing in Britain since the spring of 1976, when the Snowdons formally and finally announced their intention to separate. In that more innocent era, and since it was the first time in living memory that the marriage troubles of a senior royal had been aired, the effect was to shake the nation. Dempster had nurtured and followed the story for years, so he must have had mixed feelings about the timing. Only three days before, on 16 March, Harold Wilson had resigned as he had foretold.

The biggest scoop of Dempster's life – the sort of news that rocks stock markets and ploughs up the political landscape – was crowded out by his special subject. It is said the Prime Minister chose his moment as a favour to the Queen, hoping his news was of greater import than her sister's and would therefore attract more press. If so, he was singularly – even suspiciously – ineffective. The middle and down-market papers cleared their front pages for the royals, and Dempster found himself rehearsing all the details of the Snowdon debacle with as much frankness as he dared in a family newspaper.

Unfortunately for Princess Margaret, she had become fair game to journalists. Once she was rather well liked by the British public, for putting church and Commonwealth above her desire to marry divorced Group-Captain Peter Townsend. 'Sets' being very much the thing in those days, they hoped she would find love with one of her wealthy landed British set – Lord Glenconner's son Colin Tennant, perhaps, or the heirs to the dukedoms of Blenheim and Buccleuch – but they welcomed her modernity, too. If her life was sybaritic and centred on holidays and nightclubs, at least it revolved around fun, which seemed deserved after her sacrifice. And even though Snowdon (born Anthony Armstrong-Jones) was not exactly common, her 1960 marriage to a fashion photographer was in its way a precursor of the swinging decade, when class barriers were briefly and selectively breached, while more status accrued to the creative media types.

At the relatively late age of 30, Margaret seemed to have found happiness with Snowdon, and people wished them well. By the mid-Seventies, however, patience had worn thin. The marriage had become half-open within two years. She had been linked to Peter Sellers, the TV reporter Derek Hart, the vineyard-heir Tony Barton, the musician and writer Robin Douglas-Home* and her mother's nephew Lord Lichfield ('a kissing cousin,' she said). Snowdon had sought comfort with not only Jacquie Rufus-Isaacs but also Pamela Colin, soon to be Lady Harlech, the writer Angela Huth, his old model Jacqui Chan and a string of ex-debutante groupies at *Vogue*. But by now, he was in an affair that would eventually lead to marriage – with the television producer Lucy Lindsay-Hogg – while Margaret was dragging around a fey young man 17 years her junior.

He was Roddy Llewellyn, second son of the Olympic rider and future baronet-cum-knight Harry 'Foxhunter' Llewellyn. Since it began in September 1973, his misalliance with Margaret had been a matter of elliptical comment in the papers – and more ribald observations in the *Eye*, which broke the story. However, no news outfit yet possessed hard evidence with which to shock the British

---

* Another 'Aspinall suicide', Douglas-Home fell on hard times after his affair with the princess ended in 1967. Landing a job as Aspinall's pianist at the Clermont Club, he was sacked after selling the *Daily Express* a photograph of his employer playing with the animals at his private zoo in Kent. Blackballed, depressed and desperate, in 1968 he allowed some of his letters from Margaret to be sold in a New York auction. Dropped by all his old friends, he succumbed to shame and shot himself.

public. The pair was known to enjoy intimate breaks on Mustique, the Caribbean holiday island owned by Colin Tennant. (As a wedding present, he had given Margaret a ten-acre plot with two lodges and a villa that she named Les Jolies Eaux.) Picture editors dreamed of a paparazzo shot of the lovers *in flagrante*, or at least swimwear.

But while Tennant turned reporters away at the airport, the press had to hold its peace. That all changed in February 1976, when a New Zealand-born journalist posing as a vacationing teacher staked out the beach bar on the island. Eventually, he managed to snatch a picture of Margaret and Roddy among friends, sitting next to each other in their beach clothes.

Shorn of the surrounding group, billed as 'proof' of their romance, the image sold round the world, and in Britain provided Rupert Murdoch's *News of the World* with an excuse to abandon euphemism and tell all. It was also an excuse for which Snowdon had been waiting. Unhappy with his role as consort, he had been living a virtually separate life from his wife for some years – but while they were still under the same roof, the discourse could get a little stormy. On one occasion, he was found on the battlements of a royal palace because it was the only place he could 'get away from the bloody woman'. Another time, he left a note in his wife's glove box reading 'You look like a Jewish manicurist' – and in her bedside book, the message 'I hate you.' Sensing a media-friendly opportunity, in five days Snowdon pressed for and obtained a separation agreement, then left for Australia on a prearranged trip to plug an exhibition and book.

It was said that Roddy was the first of Margaret's lovers to get under his skin. Snowdon called the boy – who was similar in looks, but giggly rather than withering – a 'lightweight'. When Roddy met the 43-year-old Margaret, he was 25, sexually confused, burdened by neuroses and virtually unemployed. Having lodged in London with decorator Nicholas Haslam – and left after a catfight – he was now staying with his brother Dai. While he earned some pin money as a genealogist at the Royal College of Arms, he relied on a family trust and a small inheritance to survive. Crucially, though, he was a 'spare man' – and Colin Tennant needed one for a five-day house party in Glen, his baronial pile in Peeblesshire, at which the unaccompanied princess was to be his guest of honour.

Tennant found Roddy through his great-aunt, the hostess Violet Wyndham, who had met the well-born drifter with Haslam. Offering to cover his travelling expenses, the fretful host persuaded Roddy to pack a dinner jacket and join the party. The plan was to rendezvous with the other family and guests, including Margaret and her two children, for lunch at the Café Royal in Edinburgh, then depart for a week of walks and picnics in the Borders, broken by a visit to the capital's annual Festival.

Margaret was immediately taken by Roddy, and showed her charming, humorous side. He, no doubt flattered by her attention and enticed by the pampered life she could offer him, was up for the adventure. Before driving to Glen she bought him some Union Jack swimming trunks in Jenner's department store, for use in Tennant's outdoor heated pool. After dinner and a singsong round the piano, they spent the first of many nights together.

Since, by virtue of his upbringing, Roddy had brushed up against smart sets before, acceptance in this lofty circle understandably went to his head. He had grown up in the shadow of his playboy brother Dai, whose schooling and lifestyle only served to emphasise his lowly position as younger son. While Dai went to Eton, Roddy failed the entrance exams and suffered five years at Shrewsbury. Although the breeding ground of *Private Eye* and in part the model for its satirical school St Cake's, Roddy found it insufferably hearty. (But then his favourite bedside reading was *Burke's Peerage*.) At their father's Welsh estate, while Dai was at ease on horseback, Roddy preferred raising cacti in one of the glasshouses.

When Roddy followed in his brother's footsteps and enrolled for a year's philosophy course at the University of Aix-en-Provence, Dai arrived one weekend in an open-topped sports car, with an invitation to the Monaco Grand Prix and the baronet's model daughter Caroline Blunt beside him. It was 'typical,' Dempster later wrote, 'a vignette of the years to come, producing in Roddy a sense of inferiority and insecurity – Dai, with money to burn, a fast car and a pretty, sexy woman, while he traipsed along unable to make an impression.'

The humiliations continued. Roddy didn't lose his virginity until he was 22. He was too small to join a Guards regiment, and had to be found work first at

Harry Llewellyn's electro-plating business in Newport and then at the Tennants brewery in Sheffield. (His father was a director of its holding company, Whitbread.) When he transferred to head office in the City of London, he became depressed and resigned within three months.

Nor did his prospects improve: partnership in a mobile disco produced so small an income that he abandoned it for genealogy and – briefly – a part-time job in a gallery on the Fulham Road, owned by the fashion designer Piero de Monzi. To have been plucked from this trough and cherished by a princess – albeit an ageing and voluptuous one – seemed a miraculous turn of events. Returning to London, he burst into the fraternal flat and declared: 'I've just had the most wonderful week of my life!'

Margaret seemed to feel the same way. Despite reservations among her more conventional friends, she arranged further assignations at the homes of the Tennants and others, who would hold dinner parties to accommodate her and her 'darling angel'. She constantly telephoned and wrote to him; she advised him on the decoration of a little basement flat in Fulham, bought for him by his parents; and in February 1974, she flew him out for a three-week holiday to Mustique.

It was, in Dempster's words, 'almost a second honeymoon and did not have one jarring moment'. By day, the couple stayed in their compound, occasionally venturing out for picnics and afternoon swims in the sea. By night, they drank whisky, listened to the World Service, played board games and expanded their repertoire of songs. But their liaisons were never again to be quite so carefree. Both were concerned by the disparities in their age, wealth, status and sexual appetite, and constrained by her public life. And if the next six months passed well enough – with a return to Glen for their 'first anniversary' and a subsequent weekend at Roddy's parents – melodrama was waiting in the wings.

***

In an effort to improve Roddy's finances, Margaret asked Colin Tennant if he could find her boyfriend some better paid work. Tennant obliged by approaching the millionaire businessman Algy Cluff, who – mindful of mutual back-scratching – offered Roddy a post as his personal assistant. But as Roddy later told Dempster, he was ill-equipped for the world of high finance: 'It was obvious to everyone at Cluff's that I didn't have a clue what was happening. I was hopeless from the beginning and didn't know what anybody was talking about… I was whisked around the City all day by Rolls, and occasionally asked to produce pieces of paper. Perhaps I could have made something more of it, and enjoyed it more, if I had been helped along.'

That sense of helplessness had a traumatic effect. Two months into the job, Roddy left for lunch – and did a bunk. He went home and packed a case. After telephoning his mother and Margaret, he put his keys and a note through a friend's letterbox and headed for Heathrow, intending to catch the first plane he could. His original destination was only Guernsey, home of his mother's family, but within two days he was back – having withdrawn a few hundred pounds from his bank – and headed for India via Turkey. On the plane to Istanbul, Roddy had a stroke of luck. He met an amiable fellow traveller to whom he poured out his troubles – only omitting Margaret's name – and from whom he took a spare room for the night. According to Dempster, he then travelled round Turkey by bus for three weeks and after spending a few days on the south coast, 'felt he had things "straight" in his mind and could bear to return'.

Roddy retreated to Wales, where he would later learn that Margaret had taken an overdose of sleeping pills – enough to 'cry for help' anyway. Staying at his parents' house, he began to plan a tour of South America with a friend called Louise Macgregor. Their first stop in the New Year would be Barbados, where his father had a neglected villa that he wanted to sell. Roddy was to borrow furnishings, paint the pool and – in return for a commission – find a purchaser. Some hope.

In February 1975, Margaret returned for a break to Mustique, and since the Queen was on a Caribbean tour at the time, chose not to invite the Barbados-based Roddy. He meanwhile had embarked on a rum-fuelled bender that Louise took to presage a nervous breakdown. On her advice, he began to see Dr Patrick Smith, a psychiatrist on the island, and seemed to be benefitting from their sessions together – until he was the victim of a practical joke.

It was not a good week for him. The *News of the World*, available in the West Indies, had run the first of a two-part series on the Snowdon marriage, and referred to Margaret's latest dalliance. Now he was sent an airline ticket to Mustique by an anonymous 'friend', who claimed the princess wanted to see him. However, when he arrived at Les Jolies Eaux – unannounced – he was given a lukewarm welcome. Margaret explained that not only had he been hoaxed, but her parents-in-law were staying. Since she was returning to Britain that night, she gave him a lift back to Barbados, where she changed planes and headed back to London.

Disconsolate and distressed, Roddy spent a night in Barbados before returning to Wales – via a stint in London – where he set himself the task of tidying the family grounds and greenhouses. He saw Margaret on his occasional visits to London, and she kept in touch. But for now, she occupied herself with other companions – and the further disintegration of her marriage.

Over the months, Roddy's rural recovery continued. Through Haslam he had befriended an upwardly mobile Australian male model called John Rendall (later social editor of *Hello!* magazine, and now best remembered as the owner of a pet lion). Resuming contact, he discovered Rendall was involved with Haslam's cousin Lady Sarah Ponsonby and helping her to run an upper-class commune in Warwickshire named 'Parsenn Sally' (after a breed of Swiss milk-cow). In June 1975, Roddy was invited to join their new community in

Wiltshire, based at Surrendell Farm, near Malmesbury.

The aim was self-sufficiency, with extra income provided by – and surplus produce going to – a restaurant the group opened in Bath, again called Parsenn Sally. The actress Helen Mirren, who in Warwickshire had been a regular refugee from the Royal Shakespeare Company's Stratford base, was a frequent visitor and later remembered the commune for its fancy dress parties fuelled by home-brewed scrumpy and 'five-skin spliffs'. And despite its almost total lack of creature comforts, Roddy was very happy there, supervising the kitchen garden and tending his prize sow. Indeed so enthused was he that he managed to persuade Margaret to come for lunch one Sunday, and to return for a winter weekend stay, when she mucked in with the chores.

Although the locals were to say the princess looked 'like a farmer's wife' on her visits to Wiltshire, she still had her taste for luxury and the following February took Roddy back to Mustique. The upshot was the famous Beach Bar photograph, the beginning of the end of her marriage, a press siege of the Surrendell commune (which soon fell apart, as much from internal as external pressures) and a change in the rules of reporting. Previously, the Margaret-and-Roddy saga had been like a private company in which Dempster held the majority share. The result was that, while no one could rival his knowledge of the intersecting networks that supported the business, it became effectively nationalised.

At the same time, the behaviour of the protagonists

altered. Margaret allowed herself to be photographed in public with Roddy, as if to test the tolerance of public opinion, while Roddy was seen by some to be profiting from his new notoriety. As Dempster wrote: 'Though Princess Margaret herself refused to hear ill of him, there was an increasing feeling among her friends that Roddy was abusing her trust [through] a series of cheap publicity stunts.' But Margaret stood by her man through this period, taking him to Glen and Mustique, weekending again in Wales and bringing him along to various country house parties.

True, Roddy's presence was comforting in 1978, when Margaret agreed to divorce Snowdon – leaving him free to marry his pregnant girlfriend that Christmas – but by then all passion was long spent. And if he was sincere in saying 'I don't see why things should not continue as they are forever', he was also precipitate. In October 1980, Roddy accepted an offer from Peter Stringfellow to celebrate his 33rd birthday at his Soho nightclub, inviting 20 guests to a free champagne dinner (with the press in attendance). One of them was Tania Soskin, a fashion designer turned travel writer, and an old flame of John Rendall. Now sparks flew between her and Roddy, and by the New Year a romance had been kindled.

Strangely, no one – least of all Roddy – chose to bring this change of affairs to Margaret's notice, even though it was mentioned in the *Mail*. So when he went for his last jaunt to Mustique in February 1981, she still remained unaware that she had been replaced in his affections. Only

1. Dempster, dressed in Sherborne school uniform, poses with his mother Topsy.

2. A young and rather dashing Dempster at the end of his school days, circa 1959.

3. Dempster, seated far left, at the gaming tables of *Les Ambassadeurs* in 1960.

4. Lord Beaverbrook, media baron. It was to the William Hickey column of the *Daily Express* that Dempster first contributed stories.

5. From left to right: *Private Eye* editor Richard Ingrams, Christopher Booker and actor and cartoonist William Rushton in the *Eye's* office in 1963.

6. Sir James Goldsmith and his then partner Lady Annabel Birley arrive at Bow Street Court, London, in July 1976. Goldsmith was bringing a criminal libel prosecution against *Private Eye* magazine.

7. Harold Wilson leaving Number 10 *en route* to hand in his resignation at Buckingham Palace in 1976. Dempster had floated this story a full three months before Wilson made his decision public.

8. Princess Margaret (centre) and her friends Lady Ann and Colin Tennant waiting on the jetty in Mustique to greet the Queen in 1977. The Royal Yacht *Britannia* can be seen in the background.

9. Roddy Llewellyn celebrating his 32nd birthday in 1978 at a London club.

10. Writer Antonia Fraser and playwright Harold Pinter, photographed here in 1975. The revelation of their affair was one of Dempster's biggest scoops.

11. The notorious restaurateur Peter Langan (left) with actor Michael Caine and Caine's wife Shakira, circa 1975. Langan and Caine co-founded Langan's Brasserie in London's Mayfair.

12. Dempster with his new wife Lady Camilla Osborne, outside the Hyde Park Hotel after getting married, 1977.

13. From left to right: Dempster's first wife Emma de Bendern, Audrey Hoare, Dempster and his second wife Camilla, at a publishing party in the mid 1980s.

14. Always the party man. Dempster with Joyce Blair at The Berkeley Square Ball in July 1985.

15. Dempster files a story over the phone, 1985.

16. Society photographer Lord Lichfield and actress Joanna Lumley pose in matching tweed knickerbockers in 1981. Lichfield and Dempster worked together in the early days.

17. Thierry Roussel, his wife Christina Onassis and their daughter Athina pose on the deck of their newly built yacht in 1985. Christina was the subject of Dempster's book, *Heiress*.

18. Socialite Dai Llewellyn in London in 1982. He was part of the Dempster set and a regular in his column.

19. Charles Benson and Nigel Dempster at Royal Ascot in the 1980s. Old Etonian Benson was a great pal of Dempster's and a fellow lover of the turf.

20. Sir David English and Dempster share a joke. English edited the *Daily Mail* from 1972 -1992.

21. Andy Warhol taking a photograph of Tessa Dahl in New York, July 1973. Dempster and Dahl had an affair; a rather badly kept secret.

22. Fleet Street, 1987: Nigel Dempster at the mock funeral of William Hickey after the *Daily Express* killed off the pseudonymous column.

23. Prince and Princess Michael of Kent in 1992. Dempster devoted many column inches to the Princess. Perhaps the most surprising was an article entitled, 'That's no way to treat a princess'.

24. Mohamed Al-Fayed and Her Majesty the Queen at the Royal Windsor Horse Show in 1997. Dempster reported the ex-Harrods' owner's forays into British society with wry interest.

25. Princess Diana and Dodi Al-Fayed during their holiday in St. Tropez, August 1997. The summer romance provided a filip to Dempster's faltering career.

26. Ross Benson, Fleet Street gossip columnist and long-time rival of Dempster, pictured here in 1991. He worked for the *Daily Express* for 24 years.

27. Viscount Althorp
(Earl Spencer) and his wife
Victoria Lockwood after
the birth of their first
daughter, Kitty. Spencer
used Dempster's column
to pre-empt the revelation
of his extra-marital affair.

28. Dempster, standing sixth from left, during a pilgrimage to Lourdes in
2005. He turned to Catholicism at the end of his life.

after he had confided in another guest, and been told to do the decent thing, did he break the news – which Margaret took remarkably well. Back in London, she gave her blessing to the union by hosting a dinner for Roddy and Tania, later remarking to Dempster: 'I'm really very happy for him. Anyway, I couldn't have afforded him much longer.'

Today, all Roddy will say of Dempster is: 'He was a charming slubberdegullion. No one can resist a cad.'

However, the success of Dempster's biography of the princess – much of it again at Roddy's expense – was down to luck as much as cunning. In January 1981, Dempster could write in his column: 'Rumours the romance of Princess Margaret and Roddy Llewellyn is on the rocks after seven years are, as usual, pathetically inaccurate.' It was only in April that he reported Roddy had become engaged to 'the heir to a six figure fortune' (while retaining a contract to tend Margaret's private garden at Kensington Palace).

It was Dempster's great good fortune that the book, begun two years earlier when the relationship between Margaret and Roddy seemed set to trundle on indefinitely, should have been delayed until he could report its end. In the interval, his manuscript had been passed from publisher to publisher while Dempster finished it, eventually being accepted by Quartet. This house, owned by the Palestinian entrepreneur Naim Attallah, was as well known for employing pretty girls from 'good' families as for its patchy list. Now it had a bestseller on its hands.

***

The book, serialised in the *Mail*, was a red rag to Jocelyn Stevens, who was now managing director at the *Express*. Since his days at *Queen*, Stevens had been a friend of both Margaret and her husband, and a wary observer of Dempster's intrusions into his sphere. For many years, he had been a figure of fun in *Private Eye's* Grovel column. Now, he took a page of his own paper to pour scorn on the biography. He pointed out a slew of mistakes that related to him. His wife was not a baronet's daughter and he never said to Snowdon, 'You must have some bird!' He did not direct a home movie in which Margaret impersonated Queen Victoria, nor did the Stevenses and Snowdons have an audience with the Pope. His sister had never refused to invite Roddy to her annual July dance in Suffolk because she did not hold one. 'And so on and so on... '

'*Falsus in uno, falsus in omnibus*,' wrote Stevens, who finished with a flourish: 'In the Acknowledgements, Mr Dempster thanks me for introducing him to Princess Margaret. I cannot remember performing such an unfortunate function but, if I did, I owe Princess Margaret an immense apology for which I do not expect to be forgiven.' Still, Dempster had the last laugh. Within a week – as he crowed in his column – Stevens had been removed from his post. Blamed for his papers' poor sales, he may have reflected that with a better diarist on board, and a book like his to serialise, the circulation might have been healthier.

The next year was a good one for Dempster. He raised his public profile by running in the second London Marathon. (After contracting cramp 100 yards from the finish, he only managed to limp across the line when he was 'spurred on by various missiles and the encouragement of well wishers'.) And he was enough of a name to be taken on the inaugural journey of the refurbished Orient Express from Victoria to Venice – which prompted some paid-up passengers to resist the opportunity, despite the £500-a-head cost. Among those who risked his company were Liza Minelli, a duchess, a princess, plus the 'confirmed bachelor' Earl (John) Jermyn and his travelling companion. The future Marquess of Bristol – who would become another of Dempster's regular cast – distinguished himself by refusing to move from his dining table, so that Minelli's party of six could be seated in comfort.

The diarist seemed omnipresent. He was there to point out his old girlfriend Carolyne Christie's eight-and-a-half year relationship with Pink Floyd's front man Roger Waters, when they appeared together for the first time in public, on the red carpet at the premiere of the concept-rock film *The Wall*. He had the latest news on Claus von Bulow, accused of killing his comatose wife (later acquitted). When Prince Charles' valet, Stephen Barry, sold his memoirs in New York, Dempster could report a review at the intelligence service MI5. When the circumstances leading up to the recent Falklands War were investigated, he could predict – accurately – that 'the Franks Inquiry will totally exonerate the cruelly deposed Foreign

Secretary Lord Carrington from the blame which he honourably accepted by resigning from his £27,825 post.'

Poacher or gamekeeper? One turned the other? At this period of his life, Dempster was not so much sitting on the fence as leaping from side to side and turning cartwheels on the top bar. He made friends and enemies according to his own rules, their compliance – and his likelihood of bumping into them. Once a month, he would have lunch with Nicholas Haslam at Bibendum, where he would swap favourable mentions in his column for morsels of scandal. ('If you're discreet with a gossip columnist, you don't get anything back,' observes Haslam, sagely.) Racing driver James Hunt was given good press, as was the TV boss Peter 'the Cad' Cadbury. Bianca Jagger was, but her husband Mick was not. And the polo player Luis 'the Bounder' Basualdo got both.

In his self-appointed guise as chairman of Fortune Hunters Inc, Dempster appreciated Basualdo. As a journalist he cherished him. Supposedly tutored by the great Latin lover Porfirio Rubirosa, the Argentine heartthrob had arrived in Britain to play for Cowdray Park, but in 1972 eloped with Lord Cowdray's 18-year-old daughter Lucy Pearson, by whom he had two children. For several years, the heiress paid for his polo team – Prince Charles was a member, and Basualdo acted as a royal procurer – and when they divorced, she gave him a £220,000 payoff. Now 'the Bounder' was working in the questionable role of *homme d'affaires* to the considerably richer Christina Onassis, and Dempster was delighted. Morality was a moveable feast to him. What's more, once you were in his column, it didn't matter if you were a chiseller or a swell. You were subject to his whims. Thus he might hound the disgraced Lord Lambton, who had exiled himself in Tuscany, but fawn over the Duchess of Devonshire.

The immensely wealthy Tony Lambton had been a source of irritation to many journalists since 1970, when his father the Earl of Durham died. In order to continue his career as an MP, the then-Viscount Lambton renounced his titles. However, serving as a junior defence minister in Edward Heath's government, he insisted on being known as 'Lord Lambton'. In 1973, his liaisons with prostitutes were revealed after the husband of one Norma Levy tried to sell pictures of him in bed with his wife. At the same time, a police search of Lambton's home uncovered a small amount of cannabis.

This wasn't exactly the Profumo Affair, but it was enough to force Lambton out of politics. (Having given all sorts of excuses for his tastes, he settled on 'People sometimes like variety, it's as simple as that.') Leaving his wife and six children in England, he decamped to Tuscancy and outside Sienna bought a house, grounds and hamlet originally built for Pope Alexander VII. He lived at the palatial Villa Cetinale with his beautiful mistress Claire Ward, and from there administered his British estates.

A little despotically, it turned out. A few years later, Dempster aired the grievances of the villagers of Plaworth, in County Durham: Lambton owned the deeds to their village hall, and his agents wanted £1500 to rescind a temperance ban that forbade them serving alcohol on social evenings. Repeating allegations that he was 'mean' and 'stingy', Dempster guessed the wealth of the *soi-disant* lord' at a staggering £80 million – and so received an angry letter from Lambton, complaining that such estimates put him at risk of kidnap. Dempster's reply was to print the full address and telephone of Cetinale in his column, and mock its owner for his arrogance.

Of course, Lambton was an absentee landlord who eschewed the social round. The Duchess of Devonshire, by contrast, was a national treasure – 'Debo' Mitford – who was busy preserving the grandeur of her husband's heritage by exploiting the commercial potential of Chatsworth, the family seat. The next year, when she launched her book *The House: A Portrait of Chatsworth*, the *Mirror's* diarist Peter Tory used the occasion to lambast Dempster for appearing on the PRs' guest-of-honour list alongside such worthies as the Bishop of Bath and Wells, the Duke of Buccleuch, the banker Edmund de Rothschild and the choreographer Sir Anton Dolin.

Ringing round his new peers, Tory extracted comments from Dolin – 'Oh charming. Is he going to bring Princess Margaret with him?' – and from Buccleuch: 'I don't think meeting Nigel Dempster will cause one worry or anxiety.' Adding a quote from Dempster – 'I've written about all these people in a poor light, you know' – he concluded that his rival could 'be trusted with a secret [and] this last fact, for his old fans at any rate, comes as the final damnation'.

But to some, like Ed Victor, it came as an accolade. 'You could tell Nigel something, and know that if you told him in confidence, he would respect that. In a strange way, he was very trustworthy.' And when one gossip columnist leads his page by attacking another for the quality of his connections, you have to wonder who gains. Tory's criticism only served to acknowledge his target's celebrity. He had become a byword. Describing Royal Ascot, Terry Wogan – for whom the diarist sometimes deputised on Radio 2 – called it '50,000 people in search of Nigel Dempster'.

The broadcaster-turned-PR man Michael Cole remembers Dempster back in the late Sixties, standing at the entrance to the Royal Enclosure, greeting some debenture-holders and insulting others. ('You won't get in our column, you ridiculous old bag' he would shout at the exhibitionist Mrs Shilling, mother of the milliner David.) Now, he could be found co-hosting a picnic with Nicky Kerman, who also owned the Mayfair restaurant Scott's. They each invited half the guests to a Scott's-catered feast that started in Car Park Number One with 20 in the mid-Seventies, and ended up a decade later with 300, in the less prestigious Number Six.

While he acted for all the world like the Gold Cup favourite's owner, in fact, he had a half-share in one nag, which he bought with Colin Mackenzie. At first, Dempster predicted great things for Superfluous in his column. But over three years and 17 outings, it never even beat another horse. In 1983, they switched from jumps to flat and, desperate for a win, hired Willie Carson to ride it. Superfluous finished last by a furlong, was sold the next year and was replaced by My Purple Prose, who defrayed some of the losses. In 1989, Dempster bet £50 at 200-1 that the steeplechaser could get three first places in a season, and had his confidence repaid with £10,000 in winnings.

Seldom were his wagers so successful. Dempster must have lost hundreds of thousands to horses and bookies over half a century. In his enforced retirement, says Peter McKay, 'it became quite a problem – probably because he had nothing else to do'. After the death of Charles Benson, it is said that Dempster cleared about £30,000 of his friend's gambling debts. It is also said that five years later, after Dempster's death, Ladbrokes 'realised he had got himself into trouble', and wrote off a similar sum that he owed them. Racing was clearly a thread stitched through his life. It is a surprise, then, that Mackenzie should say Dempster 'wasn't very serious' about racing – or perhaps a reflection on the speaker's dedication.

'To a certain extent, Nigel bought his way in,' says Mackenzie. 'It was funny to see him posing in front of the stands, like he was a proper owner.' But he was also renowned for his incredible largesse. 'He would always host huge lunches at the course restaurant.' Once, Mackenzie found Dempster treating the trainer of Superfluous to a bottle of malt whisky. 'What,' said his incredulous co-owner, 'are you going to buy him when he gets one home?'

With his next trainer, the young Charlie Brooks,

Dempster had an equally amicable relationship. As Brooks says, 'The owner has to like you if it's going to work. And Nigel almost took pleasure in handing over the cheques.' They met through the mother of a mutual acquaintance who looked after Dempster's retired horses – 'he couldn't bear to shoot them, so he had this mad breeding idea' – and Brooks remembers not only his generosity to the stable lads, but also his politeness. 'Every time one of his horses ran, he would send a thank you letter to the lad in charge, whether he won or lost. It's unheard of!'

In Brooks' view, 'Every owner buys their way into racing. For nearly all of them, it's an expensive hobby. But very few of them are as good losers as they are winners – and Nigel was the best.' In Brooks' estimation, he was a 'weekend London racegoer', but he smiles to think of the 'childish excitement' Dempster took in his beasts and the rash advice he took in his gambling. 'Nigel was prone to "experts" and theories. He was a crazy gambler, making each way bets at 9-4. He saw the whole thing as an excuse to spend money.' Once, they had a horse in a race at Worcester. 'I said to Nigel: "Look, it's not the day. We'll just give him a run." And the next time I see him, he's in the betting ring, shovelling money on it.'

In the opinion of Christopher Wilson, last encountered fighting his rival at racecourses: 'Dempster modelled his character on a cross between Charles Benson's easy charm and the itchy snappishness of another Old Etonian, Richard Berens, ex-editor of William Hickey and a former boss. He learned about horses from both men – and the turf was his passport to a life above and beyond being a hack that was his private dream. Dempster wanted to be a gentleman, not realising there's no such thing as a gentlemen journalist – the perfect oxymoron – and the turf was where he believed he had separated himself from the common herd.'

Taki says that when you went to the races with Dempster, 'it was like being with a rock star. He knew everyone and everyone knew him – owners, trainers, broken down jockeys, everyone.' Brooks notes 'he was an object of fascination'– and he loved both being the centre of attention and making himself so – but at every course 'he went out of his way to make friends'. The bonhomie had its perks. ('He had the knack of getting Sheikh Mohammed to give him the odd horse.') But the motives, thinks Brooks, were neither social nor professional.

If National Hunt racing had once been the preserve of the Eton-Oxbridge-Guards brigade, 'that all changed with the Lloyds crash,' says Brooks. From the mid-Eighties to the early Nineties, when their insurance syndicates called in personal liabilities, the losses sustained by the established upper classes rearranged the hierarchy of Britain just as much as the City's 'Big Bang'. The money shifted to a new breed that Dempster the diarist disliked. 'Spivs', he called them in interviews. But he had no qualms about their company at the course.

'He wanted to leave his job at the gate,' says Brooks, 'and if that wasn't always possible, he tried. In the 15 years I knew him, he never once asked me about anyone who appeared in his column. He compartmentalised his life, so that racing – which was his passion – could be his escape.' And all things considered, says Brooks, 'the horses didn't do too badly. Aardwolf and Switch won a few – even in France, which isn't easy.'

POMP
The Former Greatest Living Englishman

D empster certainly 'got one home' professionally in
1982, though it did him no favours in the long run.
While he advertised the harmony of his own marriage –
Camilla had adopted a python at London Zoo and called
it 'Nigel' – he was among the first to detect discord in the
Waleses'. Originally making his allegations in July – in
a segment on American television's *Good Morning America*
to mark the first anniversary of the royal wedding – he
would be roundly reviled for it.

A regular on this programme and generally unscru-
tinised by his British peers, Dempster would throw
caution to the winds when he appeared – not only giving the
impression that he was intimate with the Royal Family, but
making outlandish claims about them. He famously started

a false rumour about the paternity of Prince Andrew on one occasion (and when Christopher Wilson discovered it, bought his silence with 'quantities of Mâcon Lugny'). This time, he described Princess Diana as 'a fiend and a little monster', and claimed she had banished Prince Charles' friends from Kensington Palace, leaving him 'desperately unhappy', knowing that 'he can never divorce her.'

He went on to say that Diana disliked polo and had broken up a dinner party for colleagues from two of Charles' teams by throwing down her napkin and sighing 'I've never been so bored in all my life.' And in November, he used his *Mail* column to disclose that there were 'problems in the couple's 16-month marriage': although Diana was uninterested in her husband's field sports, Charles had spent the last four Mondays in a row chasing foxes.

The next month, these allegations were raised again on the London TV show *Bennett Bites Back*, prompting furious comment from the gutter press. The *News of the World* gave over its front page to an editorial. 'It will not be long before Dempster is off again on his travels,' it concluded, 'probably to the rented home he enjoys so much on Long Island, outside New York.' (This may have been an inaccurate attempt to warn off Dempster, by hinting at his relationship with Tessa Dahl.) 'The Princess of Wales – and all of us who love her – will be hoping that he has a good long rest.'

At the *Daily Star*, its royal correspondent Andrew Morton was also currying Diana's favour. 'Monsters don't weave magic,' he wrote soppily. 'It is inconceivable that she is leading a Jekyll and Hyde existence. Pretty in public, pouting in private – NO.' Two days later, Morton turned up a witness to Diana's affability at the contentious dinner party. But no mention was made of her bulimia, which Dempster also claimed as a scoop.

Broadly, he was right. And he was way ahead of the pack: *Vanity Fair*'s Tina Brown didn't write that Prince Charles was 'pussy whipped' for another four years. Still, he had been outflanked. To have his facts disputed was nothing new, but the rancour flowed from new pens. In the wake of the Wales wedding and the 'Diana effect', the Fleet Street papers now had journalists dedicated to royal reporting. These were full-timers, in cahoots with the increasingly spin-conscious 'Firm', given space outside the gossip columns, and careful not to upset the people's princess too much.

Though it could be argued Dempster had behaved no more nobly when working with Margaret, there was a difference of degree. Dempster maintained the polite fiction that his book had been written without its subject's co-operation. And unlike Morton's later biography of Diana, his was not part of a pre-planned PR campaign in the run-up to a divorce. As for devoting himself to covering the royals, the travel required by a correspondent's job would have suited neither him nor the *Mail*. He was better off as figurehead, writing about his own generation*. Perhaps

---

*The younger set was left to the likes of his assistant Timothy Swallow, who called his boss 'Caligula'. A *protégé* of Tina Brown and the spangly anti-star of her *Life as a Party*, this middle-class boy from Doncaster became a victim of his own hedonism and committed suicide in 1983.

piqued that his some of his territory had been annexed – or blustering to buoy up his confidence – he would brag that he had never met Princess Diana.

It was not exactly wise to dismiss the biggest social story of the century before even trying to charm her. No doubt, Diana was already peeved by Dempster's disclosure that Camilla Parker Bowles and Lady 'Kanga' Tryon, 'the two happily married women who influenced Prince Charles most on personal matters' – had been left off the list at her wedding reception. Still, it did show the diarist never feared the consequences of being his own man. At least, up to a point, Lord Copper. Two spats in 1985 showed him in very different lights – though in both he adopted the role of the injured party.

The former Trade and Industry Secretary Cecil Parkinson might have had more cause than him. In 1983, he had resigned from the Cabinet after the *Eye* revealed his old secretary Sara Keays was carrying his child. Since then, gossip had been doing the rounds that the smooth Tory MP had a more-than-professional relationship with his new secretary. The Hickey column had mentioned a late-night car accident involving the pair. The *Mail* had sent a reporter to nose about Parkinson's block of flats in Pimlico – which prompted a complaint to the editor.

Parkinson assured David English, now a Tory knight, that there was no truth in the rumour, at which point – so Byzantine are the workings of some journalists' minds – the trail becomes less clear. The most likely sequence of events that March is this: Dempster believed the story was worth a punt in Grovel and – without admitting to authorship – let his *Mail* colleagues know of its imminent appearance in the *Eye*. On the eve of publication, the newspaper again contacted Parkinson, to test his reaction, and he showed no hesitation. Going to court, he obtained an injunction on the *Eye*, so that it had to withdraw most of its edition from sale and reprint with the offending paragraphs blacked out. Then all hell broke loose.

Fleet Street was pointing the finger at Dempster, whose reputation – and with it his job – was on the line. So he denied supplying the item to the *Eye*, which had been edited that issue by Richard Ingram's young *protégé* and deputy, Ian Hislop. Dempster claimed the article had merely been 'shown' to him by Hislop, and he had advised against pursuing it. The *Eye*'s lawyer had certainly been unhappy about publication, as Ingrams knew, but to have Dempster disown the piece now undermined any chance of a legal standoff.

In the past, Ingrams had always covered for Grovel's informants and writers, taking the rap himself. When Roddy Llewellyn got fed up with the malice – eventually winning a defamation case against the *Eye* – Ingrams wrote a half- serious paragraph distancing Dempster from the libels. Perhaps it is unfortunate that Hislop had been standing in for him that week: the loathing between Dempster and the 'midget' was mutual. But, liable for a hefty payout, Ingrams felt the *Eye* had been set up by the *Mail*, which made front-page capital from the story at no risk to itself. He retaliated in an editorial that categorically named Dempster as the author and said Parkinson should sue him.

Dempster, panic stricken and far from sober, rang Ingrams. He threatened to resign from Grovel if Hislop were not removed, and added that '*Private Eye* is succeeding where Goldsmith failed. It will get me sacked from the *Mail*!' In fact, he survived, but in a damaged state. Again, he had misread the times. The world had moved on. This was Thatcher's Britain now, a tougher, smugger place. While in Julian Fellowes' phrase the Sixties 'faced both ways', there was less room for these japes in the Eighties. Flouncing out of the *Eye* , where Hislop went on to be editor, Dempster condemned himself to years of feuding. And at the *Mail*, he never pulled quite the same weight.

That became apparent in July, when he was initially prevented from regaling his readers with all the background to Norman Lamont's black eye. The junior minister in Parkinson's old department had told anyone who asked that he had walked into a door, but Dempster had heard otherwise. It transpired Lamont had been thumped after being chased down a Bayswater street by an irate art dealer called Richard Connolly. The married MP had been discovered late one night at the home of Connolly's love interest, Lady Olga Polizzi. But herein lay a problem for the *Mail*. Lady Olga was the daughter of Lord (Charles) Forte, with whom the paper was already in litigation. Since he did not wish further to antagonise Forte, English would only allow an oblique account to appear. So Dempster rose to the challenge and resigned, telling the

Guardian that matters 'of national interest' were being suppressed, and advertising his services to other editors.

He spent that Monday evening at the Berkeley Square Ball and, like a deb's delight of old, commanded the stage for an amusing if incoherent speech in which he repeated his resignation, commended himself and deplored the fact that Prince Philip – who was a 'foreigner' – had opened the proceedings. The next day, he began his memoirs, and talked to prospective employers. He was spotted in the editor's office at both the *Daily Express* and *Mirror*, where he asked for his £60,000 salary to be more than doubled plus a 'transfer fee' of £250,000. (A couple of months later, he claimed he 'was quaking in his boots' lest the *Mirror*'s Robert Maxwell accept his offer.)

Over at the *Mail*, Sir David acted with his customary *sang froid*: 'He has half resigned,' he said, 'a well-known Dempster device. I expect we shall see him back.' And indeed they did. English said Dempster could print his uncensored story if he was willing to personally indemnify the *Mail* against any legal costs. ('It will prove who has the best lawyers,' he observed. 'Nigel or myself.') Dempster, who had talked to Connolly, agreed and 48 hours after abandoning his diary was back running the ship – and an unexpurgated account of the Lamont affair.* 'These poor people could at most produce one or two columns,' he said of his assistants. 'They have holidays and children – I have to think of them.'

---

* There is an unlikely story that Lamont believed 'Nigel Dempster' was a pseudonym, like William Hickey. It is alleged that some years after this affair, when he and Dempster were introduced at a Christmas party, Lamont looked confused and said: 'I didn't believe you really existed.'

On a roll, he continued: 'One era is closing and another is beginning. How can I do a column for just one newspaper when I am the greatest gossip columnist in the world? Everyone insists that I am.' Wrong headed, bloodied but seemingly unbowed, Dempster was irrepressible. Told by the *Sun* that Sir David had called him a 'real aristocrat', he replied: 'I've fooled everyone. Clearly English thinks that anyone who dresses in a suit, cleans his shoes and speaks ordinary English is an aristocrat.' It was a mercy he didn't mention – as he had in *Private Eye* – the trophies for ballroom dancing, displayed over the fireplace in the dapper Sir David's office.

***

Dempster's own passions remained the same. Racing, gambling, his daughter and stepdaughters. He lunched and drank and consolidated his empire – hiring as his deputy the able journalist Adam Helliker, who did much of his 'legwork'. He expanded it, too, in 1986 becoming diarist for the *Mail on Sunday*, which after a difficult birth in 1982 grew into an assured little sister of the daily paper. But 'to some extent,' says Nicholas Haslam, 'Nigel was trapped in a fantasy past, writing that kinsman-of-Lord-Derby type of stuff.' He may have been invited to all his parties, and to weekend lunches in the country – 'We were oddly close,' says Haslam, 'because we trusted each other' – but Dempster was sitting on his laurels now, not always aware of the changing world around him.

In the Seventies, he was the joker in the pack, his column providing light relief in a gloomy Britain riven by strikes and economic mismanagement. A decade later, he gave pleasure as a familiar friend. Aristocrats still yielded stories – selling their estates, being blackballed and cuck-olded – and Dempster was not without contacts among the rising rich. He broke the news of Jerry Hall's brief desertion of the now-divorced Mick Jagger for the pools heir and racehorse owner Robert Sangster. He revealed that the entrepreneur Peter de Savary had ditched his fiancée to marry his secretary – and then done the reverse. But, possibly conscious that he had burned his bridges with Princess Diana, his thoughts drifted too often to the supporting cast in the royal soap opera – and in the case of Princess Michael of Kent, perhaps his judgement suffered.

These days, the six-foot Princess Michael seems to have secured some cachet. The artist Tracey Emin calls her 'a true Bohemian'. Her son Lord Frederick Windsor is a fixture in fashion and thespian circles. But in 1983, the Czech-born Catholic baroness, daughter of an Austrian SS officer, was a figure of fun. Christened Marie-Christine von Reibnitz, she was known in *Private Eye* as 'Mrs Tom Troubridge' – after her first marriage to an Old Etonian baronet's son – and in the popular press as 'Princess Pushy'. Allegedly, the Royal Family nicknamed her 'Our Val', because of her Valkyrie-like qualities.

Prince Michael's wife of five years was accused – not least by Dempster – of freeloading, outspokenness and being 'more royal than the royals'. She wasmocked for learning to ride sidesaddle in Rotten Row, supposedly in emulation of the Queen. And when Princess Margaret's son Viscount Linley was asked by a magazine what he would give his worst enemy for Christmas, he replied, 'Dinner with Princess Michael'. Now Dempster was invited to lunch – and subsequently disgorged an astonishing defence of his old victim.

In a full-page article entitled 'That's no way to treat a Princess', he began by repeating two stories supposedly doing the rounds at Court. In the first, 'M-C', as he called her, was said to have annoyed the Queen one Christmas by complaining that the rooms at Windsor Castle allocated to her family were not grand enough. In the second, she was supposed to have called the police when schoolchildren disturbed her sleep by gathering under the wrong window at Kensington Palace to sing 'Happy Birthday' to Princess Diana. 'These stories', wrote Dempster, 'are at best apocryphal, at worst maliciously cruel. Princess Michael denies them vehemently, and I tend to believe her.' He went on to praise 'this strikingly handsome woman' for performing royal duties unpaid, for transforming her 'timorous' prince into 'an outgoing character with a growing rapport with the public', and for 'being more charismatic than the likes of Princess Anne'.

But even if true, his fawning over the princess was fairly emetic stuff, and at odds with the man who posed with a voodoo doll for another feature called 'Me and My Enemies'. It lacked humour and, devoid of direct quotation, the intimacy expected of a diarist. One can only assume that Dempster was flattered, charmed or smitten. Henceforth, 'M-C' and her husband received nothing but favourable coverage from him.

In the case of Prince Andrew and Sarah Ferguson, he was faced with an equal if different challenge. The divinity that hedges a monarch – or her heir presumptive and his virginal wife – did not extend to Andrew, whose taste for fast girls had already seen him dubbed 'Randy Andy'. Sarah 'Fergie' Ferguson was known to Dempster's readers as a chum of Princess Diana and the long-standing girlfriend of an older man, the motor racing figure Paddy McNally, with whom she had set up home in Switzerland. So established was this three-year relationship that in August 1985, Dempster predicted their wedding in print. However, on 3 January 1986, McNally was to tell him: 'We have decided to go our separate ways.' Dempster reported that 'red-haired, freckled and fun-loving, Sarah Ferguson has joined "old mate" Prince Andrew at Sandringham' – she was acquainted with the royals through her polo-playing father, Major Ron – 'while the man she almost married is skiing in Switzerland.'

Today, Fergie says that it wasn't exactly helpful to have her stay advertised 'while I was trying to nab me prince'. Later that month, however, as rumours of an engagement began to circulate, Major Ron informed Dempster: 'There is no prospect of such an outcome in the near future.' But within two months, the diarist had a world exclusive of just such a result. The media tried to be ecstatic –

hoping this royal romance would help sell as many papers as that of the Waleses – but could never be quite as enthusiastic about jolly, silly Fergie as they had about the primary school teacher-turned-princess.

Sarah brought out a skittish side in Diana. They prodded race-goers with their brollies at Ascot, they dressed as policewomen and tried to crash Andrew's stag party at Annabel's. A photograph emerged, showing Sarah bent over a long, hand-rolled cigarette. Foundations for the scandals that would engulf the future Duchess of York were being laid before she even left for her honeymoon in an open carriage. Inside the vehicle, Prince Edward had placed a huge teddy bear, and on the back he had attached helium balloons and a fake satellite dish adorned with the message 'Phone home'.

Such gratuitous goofiness didn't weigh with Dempster at the time. Of far more concern – genuine, according to friends – was 'the penetration of narcotics… in the top economic section of society'. The previous year, in a series of articles prompted by the death of a friend from his deb days, he had condemned the dangerous new fad for fixing heroin and snorting cocaine, laying the blame on 'the so-called swinging Sixties – in my view the most disastrous decade of the century for this country – when it became fashionable, indeed mandatory for the upper class young to mingle with the working class meritocracy in the world of show business, hairdressing, pop music and television'.

If it escaped him that he was a beneficiary of such social osmosis, it didn't lessen the impact of the first-person stories that he told – of pretty super-Sloanes who spent years 'on the spike', bringing untold misery to themselves and their families before 'cleaning up'. And luckily it escaped him that he had taken drugs himself. A friend remembers a Christmas party back in 1975, where a career criminal called George Wright had laced the punch with LSD and the chocolate brownies with hash – both of which Dempster gorged on. 'He was violently sick,' she says, 'and we were all terrified that he would find out what had happened. We told him he must have caught a bug. After all, he had the power to ruin us.'

In fact, in his private life there were times when Dempster could react with impressive good grace. When Demy died in 1983 – alone in a Jersey nursing home – the whole family went over for the funeral. After the cremation, his ashes were destined for La Moye golf club. Later, Dempster paid a simple but moving tribute. 'My father used to say that if when you die you own more than you can pack into one suitcase, then you have too much – and he died leaving exactly one suitcase… He had no possessions, no books, no paintings, no furniture. Golf clubs, he had his golf clubs.' More harrowing for him, late in 1986, his great mate Jon Bradshaw succumbed to a heart attack while playing tennis in Los Angeles. In January 1987, Dempster arranged and paid for a memorial service at St Paul's, Knightsbridge, attended by scores of friends from the *Queen* era. 'Jon's death destroyed Nigel,' says Anna Wintour. 'It was definitely the end of something for him.'

Behind his desk, Dempster pinned a picture of

Wintour, in memory of the old days. But the next month, he marked the demise of another character with more glee. Over the road at the *Express*, the editor had decided that his new gossip columnist, the dashing Ross Benson, could not compete with Dempster when he had to hide behind a pseudonym, and William Hickey would therefore be 'killed'*. Over 53 years, Lord Beaverbrook's creation had provided refuge and training for hundreds of hacks, some of them very good. In its time it had been almost a synonym for the best and worst of foot-in-the-door journalism. It was seen off with a mock funeral, complete with a flower-decked plywood coffin, filled with old cuttings, topped by an ancient typewriter and carried by *Express* men dressed as pall bearers.

A jazz band accompanied the procession as it made its way from the newspaper offices to the gates of the 'journalists' church', St Bride's in Fleet Street, where Christopher Wilson read the address. ('At the going down of the Sun – and of the *Daily Mirror* and *Daily Mail* – we shall remember them.') Then Dempster, attired as an undertaker, danced on the grave and flattened the flimsy casket for the benefit of his photographer – a different breed from the paparazzi whom Dempster proceeded to excoriate in a prophetic article later that year.

---

* Hereafter, the luxuriantly coiffed Benson and the rapidly thinning Dempster would each devote inordinate space in their columns to disparaging the other's efforts. Dempster called Benson 'the pompadoured poltroon' and was in turn nicknamed 'the tonsured traducer'. But unlike Dempster, Benson forbore from attacking his rival's wife. 'He couldn't bear competition,' says Ingrid Seward, 'and when I began to get television work commenting on the royals, he was so foul he made me cry.'

For some time, encouraged by their masters – and often obliged by their more publicity-hungry subjects – the affectionately-dubbed 'monkeys' had been chipping away at the conventions of social photography. Although the norm was still a personality mugging for the camera, shots that showed human foibles were beginning to appear. If someone looked drugged or drunk or silly, so much the better. Meanwhile, the photographers were becoming more insistent, and less humble. But some took it too far.

'Britain's leading gossip columnist writes a *cri de coeur*', announced London's *Evening News*. Under the headline 'Why the hounding has to stop', Dempster bemoaned the new pack of photographers, many of them foreign, who ambushed Princess Diana wherever she went. Riding motorbikes, contacting each other by walkie-talkie, they were inescapable. 'I write after the events,' complained Dempster. 'They are manufacturing news. It is the reaction of the Princess – startled, frightened, not knowing what to do or say – that is the news. And that has been provided by the photographer.'

While Dempster used the article to remind readers that the Waleses were leading increasingly separate lives, with Charles returning to the circle that the diarist knew himself – 'Nick Soames, Lady Tryon, Camilla Parker Bowles and Mrs Tommy Sopwith' – he also lavished praise on Diana. 'She is a marvellous princess and mother,' he wrote. 'She has dazzled the world with her beauty and delicacy... We are now panicking her, making her very unhappy.' If it was an attempt to curry favour with the woman he had once called a 'little monster', it did him no good. But as the tragic events in Paris ten years later were to prove, he had a point.

***

Just as Dempster claimed to have killed one fictional character in William Hickey – who would twice more be revived – so he prided himself on the birth of another. *Lytton's Diary*, starring the suave Peter Bowles as Neville Lytton, was a short-lived Thames Television drama series about a well-connected gossip columnist for the '*Daily News*', whose work uncovering scandal in high places was generally a force for good. In February 1986, a mutual PR exercise even saw 'Lytton' guest-edit the *Mail* column for a day. And since the items were provided by Dempster – a Niarchos in drug rehab being the lead – they made convincing reading. For still greater verisimilitude, however, they might have included an attack on Ian Hislop.

Since leaving *Private Eye*, Dempster had patched up his quarrel with Richard Ingrams. Although he was teased in the magazine's pages for fawning over Princess Michael, and now known as 'the former Greatest Living Englishman' and 'Dumpster' or 'Humpty Dumpster', he retained an affection for its maverick staff – Hislop excepted – and an almost proprietorial concern over its editorial direction. When he heard that Auberon Waugh was resigning to concentrate on other commitments, he must have sniffed change in the wind; and when, in March 1986, Ingrams announced he would shortly be handing over most of his editorial functions to his deputy, Dempster became aerated.

Waugh had already made his views on Hislop clear at the *Eye*'s farewell lunch for him. Referring to the editor designate as 'Hinton' and 'Driscoll' – a favourite device for conveying his disdain – he 'mused aloud', according to Peter McKay in *Inside Private Eye*, 'that this development was in tune with the *Eye*'s misguided new policy of seeking the custom of yobbo readers'. Asked later to comment on Hislop, Dempster told the *Sunday Times*, 'He knows nothing about journalism. He is not a journalist in any shape, size or form.'

It emerged that there was considerable rump of staff and contributors who were unhappy with the new dispensation. An appeal was made to the chief shareholder, the comedian Peter Cook, and a lunch convened to discuss other options. Present were Cook, Dempster, McKay and Waugh, the magazine's business manager David Cash and two other old *Eye* hands – who all proceeded to get roaring drunk. A strategy of sorts was agreed: under Ingrams' guiding genius, Hislop should deal solely with the spoofs and jokes; McKay would handle the journalistic content, and Dempster would return to the fold.

Many a slip between cup and lip. While Cook and Cash set off to confront Ingrams, McKay went home 'to await the call to greatness'. As he says, 'It was a long time coming.' The befuddled deputation was met with stony indifference by Ingrams. He stuck to his plans for the succession, and made his views of the failed coup clear in the *Eye*. In this account, the rebels were likened to the frustrated trades unionists besieging Rupert Murdoch's new plant at Wapping, where all his papers were now produced and printed: 'Hundreds of ex-*Private Eye* employees (Sid and Doris Dumpster) yesterday held a mass-lunch to protest at the "savage redundancies" recently imposed by Lord Gnome. As the massed ranks of pickets lurched out of one of Soho's leading eateries… they shouted, "Give us back our jobs, you Fascist bastard."'

The stage was set for a spat, and Ingrams was the first to oblige, calling Nigel Dempster a prat – or rather a Pratt – because of his entry in the 1986 edition of *Who's Who*. Invited to submit his details to the social gazetteer for the first time, Dempster had not only made himself look ridiculous by giving the aristocratic pedigree of both his wives, but laid himself open to ridicule by allowing it to be inferred that his real surname was Pratt. This was due to the wording of his entry, which read 'Nigel Richard Patton Dempster… [son of] Eric Richard Pratt and Angela Grace Dempster'.

Actually, *Private Eye* missed a trick here. Dempster's sister Erika says the third forename on her brother's birth certificate *was* Pratt and that at some time – she doesn't know when – he changed it by deed poll to the 'more elevated' Patton. (It was convenient that his paternal grandmother's surname began with the same initial.) Still, the joke as it stood was enough to delight Ingrams and his minions – and they didn't even need to break it.

Although the story emanated from the *Eye*'s offices, it was first published in the *Sunday Mirror* – from whom Dempster speedily obtained a retraction – and then repeated in the now-forgotten *Ritz*. A London magazine for bright young things, this was loosely based on Andy Warhol's *Interview* and edited by one David Litchfield – who was soon to receive an irate telephone call. Dempster had a thin skin. (Anthony Haden-Guest remembers joshing about his receding hair once, 'and he completely flew off the handle, really lost it'.) Unfortunately for the diarist, however, Litchfield recorded this ear bashing, which he then reprinted in an article called 'Pratt's Last Fall, or The Ramblings of a Man Who Doesn't Like Having Done to Him As He Does to Others'.

It did not show Dempster to his greatest advantage. 'So how are you going to pay for it?' he asked Litchfield. 'You're going to have to do something, buddy, because I'm going to take you to the fucking cleaners. This has gone on long enough. This is one of 20 incidents when you've written about me and been totally inaccurate. I've got them all on file, every single one of them, so this is obviously a malicious campaign. So… you are going to have to do something that satisfies me and my solicitors, and I'm ringing you up to tell you that you've made a cunt of yourself…because you are a cunt, and you know you are.'

The matter was resolved without recourse to the courts, but the damage was done. Henceforth in *Private Eye* – and to his great annoyance – Dempster was known as

'Pratt-Dumpster'. He replied as best he knew how. In future editions of *Who's Who* he made clear that he, his mother and father all shared the same surname. (Later, he added his 1987-9 slot as a 'resident panellist' on the television quiz show *Headliners*, another failed attempt to break into British broadcasting.) In his column, he laid into Ingrams, describing him as a 'pustulous reformed alcoholic' whose home life was 'Bohemian' and wife 'frumpy'. And he followed that up with a call to Mary Ingrams to tell her that the mockery to which he was being subjected in the *Eye* would be 'repaid with interest' in the *Mail*.

Things went from bad to worse (or childish to babyish). The *Eye* alleged Dempster had taken an annual £6000 fee from Peter Cadbury in return for favourable coverage in his column. Dempster sued and won £15,000. Ingrams had revenge by hoaxing him. Through an intermediary, he 'leaked' the false information that he had spent the last decade attacking Prince Charles in his magazine because he felt he should have been invited to the royal wedding. Dempster published and was damned. He retaliated by disclosing difficulties in Ingrams' marriage.

Ingrams came back with another hoax – this time fooling Dempster into printing details of his (non-existent) affair with Pamella Bordes. A former Miss India, who had dated both Andrew Neil and Donald Trelford – respectively editors of the *Sunday Times* and the *Observer* – as well as the sports minister Colin Moyniham. Bordes had lately been exposed as a high-class call girl. When the *Mail* discovered she had been consorting with a Libyan diplomat – and was in possession of a House of Commons pass, obtained for her by two friendly Tory backbenchers – the scandal took on a darker complexion. Dempster's report made him look a fool. But if there were laughs to be had from this sorry business, he probably had the last.

The Ingrams marriage was genuinely falling apart. Mary, convinced that he was having an affair, threw her husband out of their Berkshire house, before leaving herself for their holiday home in Rye. In her anger, she enlisted Dempster, who was happy to give her version of events a wider circulation through his diary. When Ingrams moved back in, it was with a girlfriend 27 years younger than him. Deborah Bosley wanted a baby and when Ingrams refused to co-operate, she found someone else to do her the service before returning to the old man's hearth. Like any gossip with secrets of his own, Dempster delighted in revealing the 'hypocrisy' of his old hero, tumbled from his moral high ground, and dwelt lovingly on the unconventional aspects of Ingrams' new coupling.

Looking back on the saga now, Ingrams speaks more in sorrow than anger. 'We were reconciled in the end,' he says, 'even though there was no formal announcement. Peter McKay* eventually got us together for lunch at the Gay Hussar, and we parted on good terms. But by then, I think he was already becoming ill. His memory – which had been phenomenal – wasn't so

* In 1994, Dempster gave credit for the peacemaking to his old publisher Naim Attallah, who was now backing Ingrams in his new venture, the *Oldie* magazine.

good.' Dempster, says Ingrams, 'had been a great help throughout the Goldsmith business – but towards the end, I think he rather lost the plot.'

In Ingrams' opinion, 'Nigel had been a very good journalist, if a not very good writer. He always wanted to put too much information in about people – who they had married and so on. He just couldn't resist it. But he had a great instinct for knowing who the baddies were.' Nor, says Ingrams, 'was he at all cynical'. Dempster believed in both the humorous and moral purpose of the *Eye,* 'and in the old days, he would have seen straight through the Bordes hoax.' But Ingrams believes 'David English put him up to attacking the *Eye*. He was told not to write for it any more, so he picked a quarrel.' Dempster may not have liked Ian Hislop, 'but I think he invented the dispute to please English.'

Still, as Wilde said, the only thing worse than being talked about is not being talked about. Dempster's fate was to be an increasing irrelevance to Hislop and his readers, which in the end might have hurt more than the name-calling.

CIRCUMSTANCE
Now People Expose Themselves

Tell that to Christina Onassis, who died in November 1987, aged just 37. Dempster's followers knew her as 'Thunderthighs', or 'Thinnerthighs', depending on her fluctuating weight. The ultimate poor little rich girl, her father was the Greek shipping tycoon Aristotle, whose affair with Maria Callas and marriage to Jackie Kennedy had made him as much an item in the diaries as the financial pages and court reports. Dominated by him – if often kept at a distance – Christina was one of the most eligible heiresses on earth, but had neither the looks nor the temperament to carry it off. A heavy-jawed girl, with dark rings round her eyes and a tendency to fat, her three constants in life were prescription drugs, suicide attempts and unsuitable unions.

When Christina's father died in 1975 – outliving her mother by one year – their only surviving child was left an estimated £500 million in business assets, cash and property which paid for a bizarre existence, chiefly led between Paris, New York, Switzerland and her private Greek island.

On Scorpios, the peasants kissed Christina's hand. It had its own bakery, underground laundry and 24-hour kitchen. There were three floodlit tennis courts, a cinema, and an Olympic-sized pool. At sea, she kept a motor-launch and a flotilla of smaller vessels. On land, there were dozens of Mini Mokes for scooting around. No luxury was wanting, as it could always be helicoptered in.

Christina disdained the main house, because it had been built for the hated Jackie O. So a cavalcade of guests was lodged there, or in surrounding villas, while their hostess had a marble pavilion of her own. From here, Christina ruled, dispensing with friends who did not fit in with her fancies. Since she took amphetamines to counteract the drowsy effects of anti-depressants, then barbiturates to make her sleep – eventually employing a nurse to administer the shots – she might fancy a 3am boat trip to a neighbouring island, where the night club would be paid to re-open so she could dance.

She was an obvious subject for a book and the man to do it was… not Nigel Dempster, but Peter Evans, formerly a columnist at the once-mighty *Express*, now an author and biographer of Christina's father. Evans was asked if he wanted the job by the publisher Weidenfeld but had reservations. He was working on several other projects, was short of time and had gaps in his knowledge. He suggested that 'Nigel should do the extra research, and we should share the credit. But I didn't mind if people thought he had written it, because it suited me that way. And the research he did was very good.'

Dempster bought to the party Luis Basualdo, a familiar member of his column's cast since his now-dissolved marriage to Lucy Pearson. 'The Bounder', who met (and slept with) Christina in 1970, had worked for her 11 years later, and his stories made the flesh creep. When she first picked him up, he was staying at the Palace Hotel in St Moritz, subsidised by the proprietor, who liked to guarantee some attractive-looking guests about the place. Basualdo told her he had a girlfriend waiting for him at another ski resort in Austria, but still went to bed with her – and gave her his phone number in St Anton.

That was a mistake. Christina bombarded him with calls, proclaiming her love and luring him back to St Moritz. There, they skied and had sex for the remainder of the season. Basualdo being a manifestly bad bet, there was no hope that Aristotle Onassis would allow their marriage – and elopement would have meant the end of any funds from that source – so risking Christina's wrath, her new boyfriend left for polo business in Argentina, while she found someone else to amuse her. But as Dempster (or rather, Evans) wrote: 'She had not quite finished with Luis Basualdo.'

As already mentioned, in the Seventies, the Bounder

Basualdo married and was divorced from Lucy Pearson. Working his way through her pay-off, he then ran up tens of thousands in debts to tailors, shoemakers and others, declaring in the bankruptcy court that he was down to his last pair of cufflinks. But somehow he survived, as his type often does – and in 1981 was finishing dinner in a Parisian restaurant with his new English girlfriend Clare Lawman, when Christina came in. They got chatting and she invited them to Scorpios, where she billeted them in the Jackie O house then ignored them for a fortnight. Sufficiently rested to remonstrate with her, Basualdo told Christina he and Clare were leaving – and she broke down in tears. She claimed that 'her doctors' said she needed constant security, and she would pay them to stay. After a display of reluctance at compromising their beautiful friendship, Basualdo asked: 'How much did you have in mind?'

They agreed on $30,000 a month, all expenses paid, plus a dress allowance for Clare. In return, he had to be at Christina's beck and call every hour of the day (and night, when he was sometimes required for sexual favours) all over the world. An executive at the Onassis head office in Monaco allegedly said, 'The only time Basualdo has to put his hand in his pocket is to scratch his balls.' In Paris, Christina rented him and Clare an apartment beneath her own in Avenue Foch, and increased his stipend by 20 per cent in return for walking her dog.

The arrangement could only last so long, given Christina's wandering eye and Basualdo's for the main chance. After she let him go, there was trouble over some $1.2 million that he had transferred from her account. But following her death, he was eventually cleared of embezzlement and settled in New York to pursue other ladies of means. Within a few years, Dempster would say the world was watching 'the death throes of a partly paid-up gigolo'. But at the time, Basualdo was a useful money-spinner for him.

Despite Dempster's ties to the *Mail*, the serialisation rights to *Heiress: The Story of Christina Onassis* were sold to the highest bidder – in this case the *Sunday Times*, whose careful readers will have noticed the material bore the copyright of Peter Evans and 'Nigel Dempster/ Pinebray Limited'. Dempster had been funneling his earnings through a tax-efficient company since 1977. In 1989, when the Christina book was published, his annual fee income was £280,000, of which only about a third came directly from his page in the *Mail*.

Not that the column was cheap to run. On top of the salaries for the diarist and his staff, at least £2000 a month was paid in tip fees for services rendered – or not, as the case may be. Dai Llewellyn earned his pieces of silver. Charles Benson did too, on occasion. But Benson and others could be simply the objects of Dempster's generosity (at Lord Rothermere's expense.) Many of his cronies were in a parlous financial state after the reversals of their Lloyds syndicates and, says one of the Friday lunch club, 'This was Nigel's way of helping us out. Sometimes, I would pass on a bit of harmless information and be paid for it. But every month or two, I would receive a payment through the post for absolutely no reason. The remittance slip would say something like "Uproar in Belgium", and I'd think: "What the hell is this about?" But when you've got Lloyds trying to take your house and you get a cheque for 250 quid, you don't rip it up.'

Doubtless Dempster's excuse for such dishonesty was that it kept his informants sweet. And to him, the sums probably seemed like chickenfeed. Eventually, he was said to receive £300,000 a year for his columns – and at the close of this decade, these still had their moments. He introduced the world to Joan Collins' new boy-friend, the Chelsea property developer William Wiggins – who she nicknamed Bungalow Bill, 'because there was nothing upstairs' – and he bade him farewell when Wiggins admitted that he wanted to start a family with a younger woman. He noted the relationship that was growing between Harrods' boss Mohammed Al-Fayed – an old friend of Princess Diana's father and stepmother – and the Royal Family: laying on a children's tea party at the polo tournament sponsored by his store, to which Diana was invited as guest of honour; chatting to the Queen at the Royal Windsor Show, where he told her about the restoration work he had undertaken on the Paris house of her 'Uncle David' (Edward VIII).

His reports also proved that Dempster was not entirely divorced from the modern world. The old connection to Carolyne Christie meant that, bizarrely, he was the first to reveal Roger Waters' attempts to disband Pink Floyd, which the lyricist had come to consider 'his' group. And when on his more familiar, titled territory, he could add true crime and real catastrophe to his roster of splicings and separations. In the late Eighties, Dempster posted regular bulletins on the travails of John Jermyn, the now-bisexual Marquess of Bristol, lovingly covering his short-lived marriage to one Francesca Fisher – who ran off with the Brazilian playboy Roberto Shorto – prior to his incarceration in La Moye prison after helicoptering into Jersey with 12 grams of cocaine. And with greater sympathy, he dwelt on the so-called 'curse of the Tennants'.

Princess Margaret's friend Colin Tennant, who had inherited the title of Baron Glenconner on his father's death in 1983, had three sons: in descending order, Charlie, Henry and Christopher. Skinny and striking, suffering from obsessive compulsions, from the age of 17 Charlie was a hopeless heroin addict, who Glenconner disinherited on his majority to protect the Tennant estates. After almost annual appearances in Dempster's column for all the wrong reasons, he would eventually die in 1996 from hepatitis, contracted through drug use.

His successor, the shy and gangly Henry, was a sweet, otherworldly sort – a transcendental meditation teacher and Buddhist – who married and produced a son before discovering that he was gay. In 1988, he took off round the world with his diminutive black lover Kelvin O'Mard (once a child film star in *Bugsy Malone*) and eventually died of an Aids-related illness in 1990, attributing it to his family's 'bad karma'. Meanwhile, in the middle of Henry's crisis, Christopher was involved in a gap-year motorbike accident in the British Honduras. After a 100-day coma – during which, a psychic apparently gave him 'distance healing' – he emerged with physical and psychological difficulties that stayed with him for years to come.*

Glenconner behaved with admirable restraint and courage throughout these adversities, but a change had come over him. In 1979, he had begun a development on the Carribbean island of St Lucia, selling out his interest in Mustique to a Venezualan millionaire. Following Christopher's accident, he put on the market his 'Great House', where he had entertained the 'beautiful people' Although his aim was to raise money for his new project, the effect was a symbolic goodbye to all that. From now on, the leading light of the Margaret Set, whose frolics were once fawned over in society columns, would often be portrayed as a wearisome and mannered eccentric.

The world was tiring of these larger-than-life characters of yesteryear – no better example being Peter Langan, whose eponymous brasserie off Piccadilly had been the scene of so many of Dempster's boozy lunches. In his trademark white suit and braces, the drunken Irish restaurateur had emerged in the mid-Sixties as an outrageous but charming *patron*, loved by such artists as Hockney, Kitaj and Procktor, who had traded works for free meals. His soaring intake of six, sometimes 18, bottles

---

* Despite his afflictions, Christopher would turn out to be the most successful of the Tennant boys – having a *Hello!* wedding, fathering children and becoming a pin-up for the mental health charity Headway.

of champagne a day had only been matched his bad behaviour – biting guests' ankles, smashing in a stupor onto their tables – and yet he became a favourite with the burgeoning celebrity class, who sought a frisson as well as beautifully prepared food at the establishment he ran in partnership with Michael Caine and executive chef Richard Shepherd.

Princess Margaret, Joan Collins, the comedian Dudley Moore – all had been abused or discomfited by this large, sweaty, kamikaze alcoholic. His party trick was to stand on a table and sing or declaim while dropping his trousers – and inevitably crashing to the floor. When Jon Bradshaw wrote a novel, he dedicated it 'To Peter Langan – Unfortunately for him, his dreams came true.' When Langan threw up in the swimming pool at the Hotel Cipriani in Venice – even though he was Louisa Dempster's god-father – the diarist was on hand to record it. But when he died in December 1988, the story was too big for a diary.

After a year's sojourn in Los Angeles where he had lost friends and money trying to found a Californian branch of the brasserie (which eventually opened on the strict condition that he was not allowed to enter), Langan had returned to Britain to find himself estranged from Michael Caine – and more importantly, from his long-suffering wife Susan. Had he lived, Langan would probably have been charged with attempted murder and arson, since he had tried to kill himself and Susan by burning down her house while they were both still in it. Comatose, with 25 per cent burns and damage to his brain, lungs and kidney, he survived for six weeks on a life support machine without regaining consciousness. There was no one at his bedside when he died and contrary to his instructions – he had requested no mourners – only three people attended his funeral.

***

Langan's demise was not the only upheaval in the established order. The newspapers were leaving Fleet Street, spreading out across London, and in January 1989, the *Mail* joined the exodus. The daily and Sunday papers moved into the shell of the old Barkers department store on Kensington High Street, to quarters that declared in every inch of their nylon-fibre carpet that this was a new age of style, sobriety and efficiency. Even if you wanted to dangle an employee over the street, you couldn't open the windows. There were carp ponds in the marble-faced atrium, twin glass lifts, a terrace of full-grown trees, a Zen garden and a waterfall. While Lord Rothermere transferred the intricately inlaid wooden boardroom from his ancestral headquarters to the sixth floor – including the bust of Napoleon, hero of the *Mail*'s founder Lord Northcliffe – his workers were confronted with colour-coordinated chair schemes and computer-cabled plastic desks.

The journalists had to find new places to refresh themselves. Instead of pubs, the *Mail*'s neighbours were now clothes shops, chemists and opticians. At the bars within walking distance, the hacks jostled not with their own kind but with students and estate agents. There were a few first-rate restaurants, Kensington Place and Launceston Place among them. Foxtrot Oscar, an Eighties establishment where Dempster's friend Michael Proudlock had recreated a New York lunch-spot, with tiled floors and pot plants, a simple menu on a board and racing on the television, was only a drunken drive away. But this was not the gossip columnist's natural habitat. Dempster was a 'seven minute run' from his house, but a million miles from his tribal home in the centre of London, and like many of his generation, he felt slightly adrift.

You could still count on him to act his part though. He put in another appearance in court, where he again escaped disqualification for drink driving in an almost carbon copy of his first case. And at the US launch of *Heiress* he took the opportunity to demonstrate that the spirit of El Vino's lived on. In New York, the two most powerful women in magazines had rallied round him. His old friends Anna Wintour, now editor of American *Vogue*, and Tina Brown, now editor of *Vanity Fair*, invited 150 guests – socialites, journalists and people with connections to Christina – to a lunch in his honour. When it was time for his speech, Dempster sprang to his feet and laid about him with abandon.

According to an article by Jessica Berens in *Tatler*, he pointed to Luis Basualdo and claimed he had murdered Christina to avoid repaying the money missing from her estate. 'As Basualdo stood up and triumphantly waved his arms around in the manner of a member of Everton FC, Dempster turned to [the Greek playboy] Danny Marentette and presented him as the man who had relieved Onassis of her virginity. As the English contingent shrieked with laughter, the Americans walked out...'

Tina Brown, who 'immediately had to hustle people into conversation', now says that Dempster was 'quite upset' by the New Yorkers' reactions. 'He completely misjudged his audience – this wasn't the Coach and Horses crew who would understand his cultural references'. At the time, Berens divined a 'thanatoid' instinct. However, she went on to opine that, this outburst notwithstanding, Dempster was not the man he was. He used to score 'high points on the Annoyingometer' but his page had become 'unthreatening to the point that people ring him to announce their divorces and the Hairband Squad fall over their Russell and Bromleys to deliver dippy details about themselves'. Dempster was pictured with the five Pekinese dogs that he now walked in the mornings as often as he jogged.* Mention was made of his breakfast of pink grapefruit and Earl Grey tea. He was presented as a tamed man – and to a certain extent he was. But he was also, after all, a creature of his environment. People had changed – the media had changed – and he was coping as best he could.

---

* Camilla had been breeding Pekinese since the early Eighties – which led to her husband's resumption of cordial relations with fellow canine lover Annabel Birley/Goldsmith. The latter, remembers Nicholas Haslam, held 'hilarious amateur dog shows' at her house in Ham, with prizes for worst as well as best-behaved dog, and ugliest and well as finest specimen.

There is no doubt that Dempster grew softer as he aged. Maybe as he became rich and famous, he became more forgiving of those in the same position. Maybe, as Richard Kay says, 'if you edit a diary for any length of time, you're bound to become friendly with some of the people that you write about.' The diarist's charm, after all, is not entirely superficial. But only Dempster would trumpet it so loudly. A typical item in 1989 described how he had been schmoozing with the *Sunday Times*' Andrew Neil and the film director Michael Winner, 'talking over old times, especially when [Winner] was a gossip columnist on the *Evening Standard* and helped invent a fictitious debutante called Venetia Crust, who became widely quoted in other Fleet Street columns.

'Alas, Venetia was exposed as a hoax and several journalists, including Winner, lost their jobs over the jolly jape, which ended after Venetia's coming-out dance was announced in the *Times*. Recounting events, Winner said it happened in 1958, while I felt sure it was a year later. We bet £1000 on the outcome and yesterday morning a chastened Winner called me. "You're right. I shall donate £2000 to charity as a penance – to the London Hospital Whitechapel Children's Unit Appeal, of which I am a trustee."'

The flaunting of the won't-notice-it bet (a month's take-home pay to a junior journalist); the self-congratulation that its proceeds went to charity; the name-checks for his powerful friends; the plug for a good cause; the nostalgia for the deb years; the howling insignificance of the episode: it's all classic mid-period Dempster. He could only sink lower with his gratuitous plugs for his latest book, an alternative social gazetteer called *Nigel Dempster's Address Book*, which gave potted biographies of 400 of his cast from the last 20 years. But one should not be too quick to sneer.

Ed Victor – who represented him for both the *Address Book* and the subsequent *Behind Palace Doors*, a history of Windsor marriages co-written with Peter Evans – thinks Dempster should not be underestimated. 'He had an amazing knack of making people feel they were part of the world he wrote about,' says Victor, who found him a pleasure to work with. 'Of course he relished his power,' he continues, 'but he was happy with himself in a nice kind of way. A lot of the people he wrote about actually deferred to him, not the other way round. But I never found him arrogant, in fact quite the reverse. He was eager to learn, and always ready to listen to my advice. After all, I was making him money.'

In his column, Dempster still had his moments, too – keeping his readers updated on the Duchess of York's crumbling marriage and her unwise friendship with the muscular Texan Steve Wyatt, for example, or fingering Marco Pierre White for his tardiness in paying maintenance to his ex-wife. Besides, in his gentler approach, there were several factors at play, all bearing on each other – one being the success of the trade in which Dempster had been the undisputed master: gossip.

The newspapers and their colour supplements

were increasingly dominated by articles focusing on personalities instead of issues – as Tony Benn might desire – and a wider range of personalities than ever before. *You* magazine, which came with the *Mail on Sunday,* only ran stories about people (and animals), which was a great novelty at the time; and these people were not necessarily well-known. Paint-ballers, ghost-busters, English eccentrics, wacky vicars – long before the phrases 'reality television' and 'famous for being famous' had been coined, the words were being formed in Fleet Street. Meanwhile, a new type of publication was about to rewrite the rules between the reporter and the reported. The Spanish weekly magazine *Hola!* launched a British version in 1988, and although *Hello!* was met with sniggers by seasoned hacks, they had to take its two-million readership seriously. The public was clearly happy – or in possession of sufficient irony – to surrender any need of objectivity.

As the culture of deference had declined, it had become normal for interviewers to entertain readers at the expense of their subjects. Despite its limited circulation, *Tatler* magazine, whose irreverence was partly inspired by Dempster's, had been hugely influential in this. A succession of editors – Tina Brown, Mark Boxer, Emma Soames – set a fashion in biting the hands that fed them. *Hello!,* by contrast, bowed low and kissed the tips of their fingers.

There was no malice in its articles on our flashier aristocrats, minor royals and middle-ranking entertainers. Sometimes, its subjects were paid for allowing the magazine into their beautiful homes, or to take the wedding pictures. Some were even given veto over what was written about them. And if they were demeaned by the process – which in a way robbed them of any deference due – the formula proved so successful that *Hello!* was soon flattered with imitation by *OK* magazine, and the even further down-market, *Now*. The effect was to force on the traditional press a new emollience (so it could be said that the gradual change in Dempster's column was in tune with the zeitgeist) and a ceding of power. Previously, interviewees had to risk a roughing-up from their inquisitors; now they could demand to be treated with kid gloves. At the same time, they were acutely conscious of a growing trend in the media to judge the merits of publicly accountable figures by their private lives.

The impetus for this alteration, however, came not just from magazine and newsprint publishers. Spin-savvy operators, such as Richard Branson, had recognised that by identifying themselves with their businesses, they could garner publicity. Moreover, the dark arts of public relations had reached new levels of sophistication, so that PRs were employed by figures who would once have answered their own telephones to field enquiries from the press. These characters controlled the access of journalists to their clients, favouring the most malleable, and put the best possible gloss on their activities. They paid for the parties to launch products, too – now infinitely more common than the ones to launch debs.

Meanwhile, a fame-hungry new breed realised that, in

this shameless world, one could build one's profile first and exploit it later. There was a time in Britain when being in the papers was considered at best a regrettable necessity and at worst vulgar self-promotion. By the end of the Nineties, in the quest for social or financial capital, even the 'Hairband Squad' seemed to think there was no such thing as bad publicity – particularly when used in a damage limitation exercise.

True, this made Dempster's job easier, but still it drew his teeth. Take his classic territory, the marriage break-up. With rising rates of divorce, such stories had already lost some of their news value – but now, he was shocked to say, public figures were announcing their difficulties in a civilized way, before he had a chance to reveal them. 'When I started in this business in the Sixties,' he said, 'I used to expose all sorts of infidelities. Now people have learned their lessons and ring up with their version of the story first. I can't remember the last time I exposed an MP for having an affair with his secretary. Now they expose themselves. It is *the* trend.'

Never was this more evident than early in 1991, when Princess Diana's brother, Viscount Althorp, gave Dempster a scoop for which he actually must have thanked his stars. Althorp, who had been married for 16 months to the model Victoria Lockwood, rang him to confess to a one-night stand the previous March with an old flame, the journalist Sally Ann Lasson (who claimed it was one night of many) and between them all they illustrated perfectly the new rules of gossip.

On Friday 1 February, Althorp dictated a statement to Dempster. When going through 'an extremely messy patch' in his new marriage, he said, and as the result of 'a particularly unpleasant series of quarrels' with his wife, he had arranged an illicit liaison with Lasson in a Paris hotel. Now, he was 'sickened' by the affair and back with his wife. And 'a month after the birth of our baby, we are deeply in love and our marriage is the most important thing in our lives'.

Althorp's spur to such strange action had been a call from the *News of the World*, asking if he had cheated on Lockwood with Lasson. She, it transpired, had sold a kiss'n'tell account of their fling for £5000 to the paper, which needed to verify the story before daring to publish. He declined to comment – and if at this stage he had done no more, he might have got away with it. But, the viscount thought he could outwit Wapping's finest. He imagined that, if he gave his version of events to Dempster, the news would be treated sympathetically in the *Mail* – perhaps in a few diary paragraphs – and that by depriving the Sunday rag of its story, he could somehow spike Lasson's guns.

***

To put it mildly, Althorp miscalculated. A little experience as a journalist (some broadcasting for NBC) must have convinced him that he could manipulate the media. He had, after all, leaked to Dempster the news of his engagement two years before, and at his 'small country wedding' had distributed press packs to the assembled hacks. He woke on Saturday to see his account occupying the whole of the *Mail*'s front page under the headline 'Diana's brother: The affair that almost destroyed my marriage'. Far from burying the story, he had given it 'legs' – and the *News of the World* were soon back on the line, reading him Lasson's article and asking for his reaction

Foolishly, Althorp now gave them a statement, disparaging his old lover. The paper put his comments to her, she replied with spiteful gusto, and the result was a front page reading 'Di's brother used me as his sex toy'. The news spread round the world, while the *Mail on Sunday* remarked that the only person to have come out of the episode 'with increased prestige' was Nigel Dempster: 'All the time there was a halo round his head. Why? Because he was on the side of the angels. He was not guilty of intrusion. He wrote his story at the personal request of Lord Althorp who, when in trouble, sought his old friend Dempster's counsel. How much grander can you get than to have the Princess of Wales's young brother as a friend pouring out his heart to you. Do you really wonder, then, why his rivals are spitting green with envy?'

If they were, it's hard to see why Dempster should complain that self-exposure was '*the* trend'. Althorp's unprompted confession had given him his first front page in quite some time. However, he had more reason to bemoan another development in the *Mail* and other papers. 'What used to be the sole preserve of my column

– parliamentary gossip, property gossip, showbiz gossip – has spread through every page,' he told one interviewer. 'They used to be all mine. Everything was mine. I had total command of those stories. Now it's all been stolen from me and I'm forced to compete against my colleagues.' To another he complained: 'Now it's on page one. It's on page 100… there's even gossip about estate agencies.' In these circumstances, one might question if his column still had any point. His new editor certainly seemed to.

By dint of hard work, a nose for news and a shrewd understanding of both his boss and the market, the grim-faced Paul Dacre – originally recruited in 1980 – had risen to assistant editor of the *Mail* within a decade. The next year, he was given charge of the paper's London stablemate, the *Evening Standard* – and during his short tenure there, was asked to take the chair at the *Times* by Rupert Murdoch. With this offer in his pocket, he was in a position to reach for his preferred prize – the editorship of the *Mail* – and put his terms to English. Sir David, unwilling to lose his talents, found a solution by kicking *himself* upstairs. Henceforth, Dacre would edit the *Mail*, and English would become chairman and editor-in-chief of its publisher, Associated Newspapers – while still answering to Lord Rothermere, who was chairman of Associated's holding company.

The puritanical Dacre had charily observed Dempster – and vice versa – for over a decade. Their personal values were chalk and cheese, but both recognised their opposite's worth to the *Mail*: Dacre, the ball-breaking newshound; Dempster, the proprietor's pet, a brand name that defined the paper's social prurience. 'And in the end,' says the then-royal correspondent Richard Kay, 'I think they were each scared of the other. To my knowledge, Paul never went into Nigel's office' – to him it was another country – 'and the first thing I was told when I took over the diary was that I would have to sit at a desk in the main newsroom.'

Had Dempster been a younger man, he might have tried harder to raise his game. But his column in the early Nineties definitely had the whiff of the proverbial cold potato. Making much sport of James Hewitt – now widely and correctly believed to be a lover of Princess Diana – in the battle between her and her prince, he backed the wrong horse, blithely believing the assurances of the 'Charles camp' that he would no more divorce her than Andrew Parker Bowles would divorce his wife Camilla.

Nor did he make significant inroads into the new elite of sportsmen and broadcasters. Too often, Lord Lichfield and Robert Sangster were his stand-bys. His cast of foreign multi-millionaires, such as the Australians Alan Bond and Kerry Packer and the Saudi arms-dealer Adnan Khashoggi had little resonance with his readers. And in May 1992 – while the world was agog at the revelations in Andrew Morton's *Diana: Her True Story* – he was hardly covered in glory when the second story on his page was that the hamster belonging to Fergie's 11 year-old niece Alice Ferguson had died of a stroke.

No wonder, according to one of the *Mail*'s old timers,

that 'Dacre was banging his head against the wall' when he took up his new post in June. Dempster's performance would have driven the mildest man to rage. His lead stories in Dacre's first month included the following: 'Bounder' Basualdo was looking for a new girlfriend; a racehorse trainer was nearly 'warned off' by the bookies at Ascot (but wasn't); a clutch of nonentities went to the Stella Artois tennis tournament at the Queen's Club; Lord Valentine Cecil couldn't enter the Royal Enclosure at Ascot because he had forgotten to apply for his vouchers; an Australian socialite called Primrose Dunlop was fancy-free; and Lord Cowdray's grandson was glad not to have a title.

In Dempster's defence, one might produce his story that Princess Diana had once taken an overdose of sleeping pills – but in the wake of Morton's revelations, this was small beer – and anyway, within three months he was back to his old tricks. While the 'Squidgygate' and 'Camillagate' tapes were causing consternation abroad, one of his pages contained not only the revelation that a fawn pug bitch belonging to one Daisy Schwerdtfeger, aged seven, had been stolen from the family Fiat Panda, but also a paragraph puffing the paperback release of his *Address Book*. By the end of the year, he had compounded his errors by lending his name to a magazine – *Royal Dempster's* – which, since it was in direct competition with his own column, only lasted one issue.

From then on, it's fair to say, Dempster began a decade-long terminal decline. In 1993, two years before it came to pass, he was dismissing a Parker Bowles divorce as 'ridiculous' a 'wretched rumour [that] surfaced in the downmarket *Daily Express*'. He preferred to dwell on the antics of 'Junkie James' – the Marquess of Blandford, who had briefly fallen on hard times – and the Marquess of Bristol, back in jail for possession of heroin and cocaine. Still, he scored a couple of hits that year. He precipitated the resignation of the married Tory Transport Minister by disclosing that Steve Norris was having an affair with a magazine executive – and, when five previous conquests came out of the woodwork, elicited the wonderful quote 'I don't mind being hung for a sheep but not for the whole flock.' And for what it's worth, he was the first to hear that Bryan Ferry and his wife Lucy were to separate (also announcing their divorce ten years later). Richard Kay is a staunch defender of his old friend: 'Nigel was married to the job,' he says. But when the *Mail* announced that Princess Diana was to retire from public life, it was Kay who broke the news.

Dempster was a still a useful byline in the paper. When it was discovered that James Hewitt had kissed and told about his three-year affair with Princess Diana to the writer Anna Pasternak – the details being revealed in an all too obvious *roman à clef* – he took the credit for the front-page story ('Britain's Biggest Bounder'). But to a certain extent, he was retiring from public life, too. Of course, he still relished a liquid lunch and still loved the Turf. Peter McKay remembers walking with him to Kensington Place restaurant one day, when they heard the cry of 'Nigel!'

from a scruffy, wizened figure across the road – and it turned out to be the painter Lucian Freud, asking if he had a tip for the 3.30 at Kempton. But in the evenings, he was as likely to be seen in Marks & Spencer, choosing a ready meal, as at a glittering soirée. He was probably at his happiest cooking a fabled Sunday roast and mowing his lawn in Ham; or in the Swiss Alps, where once or twice a year he stayed with Taki at his chalet in Gstaad, walking and climbing by day, propping up the bar by night.

The gang was sliding into middle age; the jinks were not so high. Bubbles Rothermere had died the year before in Cannes, from a heart attack. In New York, Anthony Haden-Guest was knifed by a psychopath. In London, Dai Llewellyn resigned from *Voila!* magazine – which was to have been written entirely by titled folk – after one issue, unpaid for his editorship. (It duly folded.) And in Athens, Taki's boat was blown up by saboteurs.

The diarist could still behave disgracefully. When his Honda Accord – how the mighty had fallen – was in a collision with a 12-year-old cyclist, Dempster demanded £500 from the boy's father for repairs (even though young Kyle Proctor needed steel pins in his ankle). But the venom that once coursed through his veins seems to have become diluted. Taki says the rapprochement he now made with Sir James Goldsmith was engineered by the tycoon's circle, who convinced Goldsmith that he was 'losing the battle' against the diarist. (His wife Lady Annabel, who had married her daughter's father in 1978, was also instrumental.) The Goldsmiths lived on the other side of Ham Common, a coincidence of which Dempster was strangely proud. But would the young tyro have rolled over to have his tummy tickled? The mature man was grateful for an invitation to the 1995 wedding of Imran Khan and Jemima Goldsmith, even if he was on the B-list – 'kept in a holding pen', as Camilla remembers, 'with a glass of champagne'.

Not that such softening of temperament extended to his staff. Dempster was always an impatient boss. Under Dacre, he was an increasingly embattled one. His lunchtime drinking tended to make him bad-tempered – and the early symptoms of the disease that would lead to his death include paranoia and mood swings. Nonetheless, he might have behaved better to his assistant Kate Sissons. After she queried an item she was checking before publication – its exact nature is protected by a confidentiality agreement – Dempster answered by throwing a copy of *Who's Who* at her, hitting her on the shoulder. (He later claimed to have slammed it on her desk, when it may have glanced against her.)

Sissons considered resigning but after a chat with a lawyer friend – to whom she confided that Dempster would call her a 'cunt' on a daily basis – she was minded to pursue an action for constructive dismissal. She settled for a £12,000 payoff and after a decent interval renewed cordial relations with Dempster, who confessed that it was '80 per cent my fault'. A wag at the *Mail* commented, 'At least she was hit by all the right people', which amused the perpetrator, but when he was mocked for his performance in *Punch* magazine – revived after a three-year closure by its new owner Mohamed Al-Fayed – he harboured a grudge.

DECLINE
A Surfeit of Diaries

Dempster and the Harrods boss had been courting each other for some time, with the diarist's old pal Michael Cole – lately the BBC's royal correspondent and now Al-Fayed's PR man – acting as intermediary. (Cole is of the opinion that 'you only needed a paragraph in Dempster's diary and another in the *Financial Times'* Lexus column for the whole of Britain to know the news.') In 1988, the three men had lunch in Harrods' private dining-room, and when Dempster mentioned that as a sock salesman, he and his colleagues had pinched a pair a week 'to save on washing', Al-Fayed replied: 'You don't leave until you pay for them!'

More recently, Dempster had reported the Egyptian businessman's honorary membership of Emmanuel

College, Cambridge, which was granted for his charitable donations. He had been even-handed in covering a dispute between Al-Fayed and the Maktoums over the management of the Dubai World Trade Centre, despite his obligations to the racing sheikhs. When *Punch* launched another attack on him a couple of years later, he would explode: 'Fayed's going to catch it straight in the nostril. There's no way out. We're going to see the whites of his eyes, if he's got any. I'm not putting up with that crap any longer.' But fortunately for Dempster at least – given Princess Diana's imminent affair with Al-Fayed's eldest son Dodi – he needed good relations with Cole to fill his page.

Through 1995 and 1996, it wasn't that there was anything particularly wrong with the diary – just nothing much right. Stories that would have transfixed the public 20 years before, somehow fell flat. Looking back, the on-off marriage of the Yorks did have a historical interest. Lord Brocket's collectors'-car insurance fraud, for which he was sentenced to five years in jail, is significant too. Dempster was among the first to record the so-called 'It girl' phenomenon: charting the affair between Tara Palmer-Tomkinson and the trendy Danish restaurateur Mogens Tholstrup; watching the emergence of the socialite Tamara Beckwith and the model Lady Victoria Hervey (half-sister of the Marquess of Bristol). He even announced the engagement of one David Cameron, a 'would-be MP', to Samantha Sheffield – then a rather scruffy pair – though he devoted more of his allotted space to the career of the artistic aristocrat

than to that of the Tory policy wonk. But in an unshock-
able age, he had largely lost the power to shock.

In one strange area, however, he did excel: the
desperation and downfall of middle-aged women. The
tone was not crowing, but rather concerned, as he chroni-
cled the indignities suffered by Mynah Bird, Elizabeth,
Countess of St Germans and Lady ('Kanga') Tryon.

The first was a Sixties figure, supposedly the daughter
of a Nigerian chieftain, who was linked in her prime to
the Earl of Warwick, Sir William Piggott-Brown and the
millionaire John Bentley. Arriving in Britain at the age of
15, she started her professional life in a Soho escort bar,
moved into modelling and began a determined campaign
to join café society. After selling her memoirs to a Sunday
newspaper, she was dropped by her smarter friends and
attacked by the tabloid press. A cameo role in *The Stud*,
starring Oliver Tobias, did little to restore her fortunes,
and she became most reported for brawling with various boyfriends. During the Eighties, she reverted to her
original name, Rachel Ogbeyealu, found God and became
a teetotal, non-smoking celibate, flitting between Africa
and her small flat in Belgravia. It was a solitary life and
when she died, two months passed before her body was
discovered, after neighbours complained of the smell.

The second was another misfit. A one-time hippy,
Elizabeth Williams was the Bohemian Lord St Germans'
second wife, whom he discarded for the shoe-designer
Emma Hope. Divorced in May 1996, two months
later 'Dizzy Lizzy' was briefly sectioned under the

Mental Health Act. A self-confessed member of Alcoholics Anonymous, Elizabeth explained her ordeal to the *Mail* thus: 'I was in a bad state. What incensed me was that His Lordship had given a party for Emma Hope… I was with him 15 years and he never gave me a party. I rang him and called him a bastard and then I smashed my phone. I'd had enough. I went out and bought two bottles of German wine and I called my doctor. Then I drove to the Charter Clinic [in Chelsea] but they wouldn't open the door to me. I got home to find the police and ambulance outside. I knew I needed help so I agreed to go to the Priory.'

The crash of Lady Tryon (a source and friend of Dempster – and some say more) was sadder and more protracted. A girlfriend of Prince Charles before his marriage, married to one of his friends – and once equal in his affections with Camilla Parker Bowles – this amusing, pushy Australian had shown amazing pluck in her ascent of the social ladder, making her fall all the more awful. While the world watched open-mouthed as the Waleses' dirty washing was strewn across the media's lawns Kanga – who had received her nickname from Prince Charles – suffered a recurrence of the spina bifida with which she was born, and simultaneously was diagnosed with uterine cancer. Successfully braving the treatment and operations for both these conditions, she found herself addicted to painkillers; and while in a clinic to wean herself off, 'fell' from a second-floor window. Confined to a wheelchair, clearly unhinged, she claimed she had been pushed. Her husband chose this juncture to demand a divorce from her, and she too was detained under the Mental Health Act when she developed persecution mania, alleging that there was a plot to kill her.

Homeless after her divorce, she booked herself into the Ritz, where she was soon exhibiting the classic signs of alcoholism – and worse. She claimed she was going to be 'the Queen of England' and on one pathetic occasion, at a polo match, was seen pursuing the future king in her wheelchair. Getting little sympathy from Prince Charles, who now announced he had all but lost contact with her, she embarked on a journey to India with mortal consequences. Contracting septicemia there, she fell ill on her return and in November 1997, at the age of 49, died a lonely death in hospital.

That was three months after Princess Diana's death in a Paris hospital, the shocking and tragic finale to her post-divorce phase. And tasteless though it may sound, the summer romance with Dodi Fayed – which indirectly led to the fatal crash in a Paris underpass – had actually provided a fillip to Dempster's faltering career. By now, he was becoming both disillusioned with his job and fearful of losing it. He had seen Ross Benson not only downgraded and relieved of his column at the *Express*, but then poached by the *Mail*.

While William Hickey was resurrected under the editorship of the charming Irishman John McEntee, Benson was now haunting Dempster in Kensington. A talented writer and award-winning war correspondent, the old 'so-called rival' was now assigned to trouble spots and the social round – and at first brought out the worst in Dempster. Mocking his address in Ebury Street, which backs on to Victoria coach station, he would call across the newsroom: 'All aboard for the Number 17 to Wolverhampton.' But of course, a lunch settled their differences, as it dawned on Dempster he needed friends in the building, not enemies. After all, only the previous year, Paul Dacre had installed Peter McKay, Dempster's old partner at *Private Eye,* in a competing gossip column.

The pseudonym chosen for McKay showed a rare sentimental streak in his editor, as well as the esteem in which its author was held – for 'Ephraim Hardcastle', named after another historic hedonist, had been the *nom de plume* used by Dacre's own father when he had been a diarist on the glory-days *Express*. McKay rose to the challenge, with a Winchellite (or perhaps, Winchell-lite) production that daily commented on the follies of the age and fearlessly picked off high-ranking hypocrites – and in the process put Dempster's efforts to shame. No wonder he had a haunted aspect in the picture that now appeared above his page. In Melbourne at the end of 1996, he was visited by his first stepdaughter Atalanta, and told her 'he was tired of his work and tired of being a hate-figure – he mentioned how people had thrown rotten fruit and eggs at him when he was running a marathon – but he didn't know what else to do.' To his daughter Louisa, he said he should have been a sports writer.

Instead, he decided to play footsie with Mohamed Al-Fayed. In the fallout from the 1997 General Election,

the Egyptian could justifiably claim some credit for turning the British electorate against the regime of John Major,
after he implicated the Tory MP Neil Hamilton in the 'cash
for questions' affair and also revealed that his backbench
colleague Jonathan Aitken had stayed for free at the Ritz
hotel in Paris – which he owned – without declaring it in
the register of members' interests. However, within two
weeks of Labour's landslide victory, Dempster published
the first in a series of items about Al-Fayed that suggested
the 'phony Pharaoh' was not totally disenchanted with
the old order. Though he was furious with the Tories for
denying him British citizenship, he had inveigled Sandra
Howard, the former model and wife of the Conservative
MP Michael, into joining forces with him to help an
eating-disorder charity.

Next, Dempster revealed that Al-Fayed was selling the
contents of 'Château Windsor' and donating the estimated £40 million proceeds to charity. (He was the biggest
single benefactor to the Great Ormond Street children's
hospital.) And a week after that came his biggest story
for years: 'A Hug From Mohammed' read the front-page
headline, above pictures of Al-Fayed welcoming Princess
Diana aboard the *Jonikal*, his yacht at Saint Tropez. The
accompanying story disclosed that she had accepted
Al-Fayed's invitation to stay in his guesthouse in the south
of France because – in direct quotes – she and her boys
'couldn't just sit in KP [Kensington Palace] all summer'.

Dempster was tremendously excited about talking
to the princess on the telephone – the call had been

engineered by Cole, who remembers she 'hooted with laughter' as the diarist joked about 'that old crocodile Camilla' – and he ran into the newsroom, shouting, 'I've just talked to Diana!' This coup was followed two days later by the news that Al-Fayed shared with Diana (and Dempster) a passion for the Royal National Ballet – she being a patron and he the generous donor of £150,000 towards its recent renovation costs.

A month passed and to the delight of a salivating press, news of Diana and Dodi's affair became common knowledge, as she alternately teased and evaded the paparazzi of whom Dempster had earlier warned. This time, he shared a banner headline with Richard Kay – 'No Wedding Says Diana' – and reported her statement that 'I haven't taken such a long time to get out of a bad marriage to get into another one'. The 'peg' for the story was a flying visit that Dodi and Diana paid to a psychic in the Derbyshire village of Lower Pilsley, and the writers opined that the princess was in the grip of 'magic carpet syndrome', shuttling between Al-Fayed's helicopter, his green-and-gold-liveried Gulfstream jet and his 18-crew yacht in a style which the cost-conscious royals would have found hard to match.

That point was rammed home a week later, when Dempster reported that Diana and her friend Rosa Monckton had cut short a holiday in Greece, to be ferried back to Paris in the Gulfsteam. Six days later, while Diana cruised from Saint Tropez to Portofino (before flying to Paris from Sardinia), he led his column with an item describing the delights of the 'love boat', as he termed the

Jonikal. Ninety-six hours after that, Diana's life had ended.

The following day, 1 September 1997, Dempster paid tribute with a diary consisting entirely of Diana-related stories. Since virtually every other page of the *Mail* was devoted to her, his choice was necessarily eccentric: a piece on Dodi's chalet in Gstaad, where the inhabitants were 'in mourning... after preparing for the arrival this winter of the Princess of Wales with her close friend Dodi Fayed'; a brief recap of his coverage of Diana, Camilla, Kanga and Charles; a paragraph stating that Al-Fayed had bonded with the princess because 'like me, she has been abused by the Establishment'; another claiming that she might have been contemplating a property purchase in the Cape Town area of South Africa, where her brother Lord Althorp was now based; and finally, news that her first boyfriend, the gardening expert George Plumptre – also living in Cape Town – 'was still coming to terms with the news and did not wish to say anything'.

****

Thereafter, as Dodi's father dealt with his own monumental grief, Dempster had little more he could say about the ill-starred association of the houses of Windsor and Fayed. He returned to the 'Chateau Windsor' sale at the end of October – it had been postponed after Dodi's death, and now all proceeds were to be diverted to the Dodi Fayed International Charitable Foundation – and the following week disclosed that, before his son had even met her,

Al-Fayed had offered Diana a job as director of Harrods International, a role for which she suggested her step-mother Raine Spencer. But then came the offending *Punch* article, and Dempster's equally offensive re-action*.

A year later, reporting a broadcast made by the Harrods chief on Arabic radio, Dempster called him the 'egregious Mohamed Al-Fayed', whose claims over his dispute with the Dubai royal family had been 'greeted with howls of derision'. He went on to cast aspersions on his old source's honesty, touched on Al-Fayed's allegations that the British were 'racist' and that there had been a conspir-acy to murder Diana and Dodi, then quoted one Laurie Mayer, who had replaced Michael Cole at Harrods: 'Mr Al-Fayed stands by everything he said in the broadcast. And if you write anything, he says he will expose you for con-flict of interest and your friendship with Sheikh Moham-med [of Dubai] and the hospitality you have received.'

The response was not entirely edifying. 'Let me,' Dempster wrote, 'help Fayed in his blackmailing ways. For the past five years, along with perhaps 100 or so of the world's press, I have reported from Dubai as a guest of the racing mad Maktoums, who have promoted the $4 million World Cup horse race... And I hope to be back there in March.' The news must have brought a wry smile to his ex-deputy Adam Helliker. Over their 16-year association, he had often incurred Dempster's wrath by questioning

* As was his wont, in 2001 Dempster patched up his quarrel with Al-Fayed over a lunch.

the public's interest in the racing figures he covered so assiduously. When their paths parted, it was with a fight that not only transfixed their colleagues but made the front page of the *Mirror*.

Helliker, a small bald man with the demeanour of a surgeon, has mixed feelings about his days with Dempster. 'Ninety per cent of it,' he says, 'was great fun.' And that made up for the ten per cent of bullying and belittlement. 'He was like a ringmaster. We were his performers, and we stuck with him because we loved the applause.' Nonetheless, Helliker was regularly approached by other circuses and often tempted to leave. 'Then Nigel would increase my money, or send me on a trip to Barbados, and so it carried on.' Eventually, however, the *Sunday Telegraph* made an offer he couldn't refuse and on Thursday 30 July 1998, he steeled himself to break the news.

He might have chosen his moment better. Dempster had been for lunch at Green's in Mayfair – 'there was a television there, and no doubt he'd lost on the horses' – while Helliker had fortified himself at Launceston Place. When Dempster returned, his deputy tendered his notice, Dempster asked if they could step out of the office to discuss it, and the two men walked onto the mezzanine where – beneath the ficus trees, in full view of scores of workers – an acrimonious exchange occurred. This was 'fucking disloyal', screamed Dempster. 'You are nothing but a bastard. You are a fucking nobody. I fucking made you!'

'It was like the end of a bad marriage,' says Helliker. 'He couldn't accept that he was being left.' Though he forgets who first touched the other, he can confirm that punches were thrown, his lip was split, and the pair ended up rolling on the carpet. By the time a colleague had separated them and Helliker had been taken to receive medical attention, the *Mirror*'s news desk had been appraised of the situation. That night, Helliker took a call from Camilla Dempster, who was 'very consoling – we talked for about an hour and a half – and she said that Nigel could also be very aggressive at home'. Over the following days, he was offered financial support by Mohamed Al-Fayed, should he wish to pursue a legal action. But in the end, he decided to let sleeping dogs lie. Although Dempster was flippant in public – 'It is possible his mouth came into contact with my body in some way' – he sent a contrite letter to Helliker, apologising for 'a moment of madness', and when Dempster called on Tuesday to say 'See you tomorrow', his deputy 'decided just to get on with it'.

Friendships on Dempster's diary seldom survived separation. But in this case, the NCP tycoon Sir Donald Gosling took it into his head to effect a reunion. Over a five-hour lunch at Motcomb's, the pugnacious pair settled their differences – but at its end, Sir Donald had to restrain Dempster from driving away. In retrospect, Helliker accepts that his old boss's increasing irrationalities were the first symptoms of his illness, but then he and many others thought that drink had finally done for the diarist: 'He was beginning to look and sound pissed after a couple of glasses.'

The police had certainly thought so the previous year, when they followed his Honda as he drove at 50mph in a 40mph zone. He was apprehended at a red light talking on his mobile phone, and the predictable course of events unfolded: five tries on the breathalyzer, the blood test at Hammersmith police station refused and urine test denied, a ban followed by an appeal. On this occasion, however, the defence reached new heights of fancy.

Dempster hadn't known there was any alcohol in his bloodstream, as he had inadvertently downed a glass of orange juice that his daughter Louisa had laced with vodka as a party prank. (This was a surprise to Louisa, who was understandably miffed to be dragged into the proceedings.) He had been making an emergency call to his vet because one of the four Pekes in his car had fallen ill*. He had been unable to inflate the bag because he was panicking over his dog and – a revelation, this – suffered from asthma.

Now, it transpired, Dempster had a condition called 'blood injury syndrome', which even prevented him from watching violent films and made him extremely agitated in Hammersmith where, his barrister said, 'he had been told one in ten people were infected with HIV'. Calling the police procedure 'legalised vampirism', Dempster added that the phobia stemmed from boarding school,

---

* The dog did indeed die, to be followed by two more within a year. When Dempster mourned his favourite, Tulip, in his column, he provoked much mirth from John McEntee of the *Express*.

where a doctor had tried to take blood: 'He made a tremendous mess of my arm and displaced the vein'; and as a result he had been unable to play in the tennis championships, while the 'pain and horror' had stayed with him ever since. The ban was overturned and the appellant was awarded all his costs.

It was some consolation at a difficult time. In June 1998, Sir David English died from a stroke. Three months later, a heart attack sent Lord Rothermere after him. And though Dempster was on good terms with the new viscount, Vere's son Jonathan, he couldn't expect the same level of protection and affection as he had previously enjoyed from the old proprietor and his partner in print. Paul Dacre – who now took on English's roles while keeping his own – tolerated the devalued diarist. After all, Dempster still had his constituency, and in his tired way was as much a part of his paper's identity as Ronald still is to McDonald's. But the editor eyed his transgressions balefully.

Launching an attempted rival to *Hello!* – *Dempsters* magazine, for which its namesake was contributing editor – was not a particularly wise move. (Again, it collapsed after one issue.) And his latest literary effort also left Dacre unimpressed. Perhaps the author shouldn't have mentioned in *Dempster's People* that 99 per cent of his gossip-gathering was done on the phone, or written that 'after a long day, including a lot of exercise, it takes a particularly appealing function to drag me out for the evening – I cannot remember when I last went to a dinner party.'

Whatever the reason, although the serialisation rights to

this collection of essays on such old favourites as Lichfield and Snowdon had been bought by the *Mail* for a high five-figure sum, its run was now cut short. There was even talk of pensioning off the old party-animal, while retaining his byline, effectively 'branding' the page, so that others did all the work under his name. Like Hickey before him, Dempster would no longer, in Norman Lamont's phrase, 'have really existed'. That he did, in some corners, had long been considered a joke.

It could be said that at the end of the last century you hadn't really arrived unless you had been sent up in Craig Brown's spoof column for the *Daily Telegraph*, and this dubious privilege was granted to Dempster on 3 January 1998. Brown introduced the piece by repeating some of the previous year's exclusive stories remembered by the diarist in his Hogmanay column. (A 'magazine mogul' called John Madejski was in a 'trading places' documentary; the model Normandie Keith had split up with the rich kid Lucas White.) He then pretended to disclose some 'outstanding scoops which Dempster was unable to print... for fear they were simply too exciting for the general reader.' For instance:

'SCOOP: I reveal that boulevardier Johnnie Beans, scion of the Heinz Beans dynasty, who once walked out with Infuriata Hoops, heiress to the Hoola-Hoops millions, has narrowly escaped being fined £12 for parking his red saloon Volvo, registration RPG 593X, on a single yellow line in fashionable Ealing, only a few miles from world famous department store Harrods, whose owner Mohamed Fayed was the father of Diana, Princess of Wales's tragic boyfriend Dodi...'

It was brilliant. Brown captured the worst of Dempster's once-perky, now hackneyed style. But perhaps the bigger joke was that, almost 40 years after finding his curious vocation, Dempster was still famous enough to merit the parodist's attention. Craig Brown is now a regular columnist for the *Daily Mail*.

***

A weirder prank was played on Dempster the next year, by Lord Palumbo's eldest son. The entertainment impresario James was aggrieved at the coverage given to the court case he had launched against his father, over control of a family trust, and took his revenge on the reporter by plastering the environs of the *Mail* and of his flagship Ministry of Sound club with Day-Glo posters that proclaimed 'Nigel Dempster Is Bald' and were illustrated with a photograph of the victim's shiny pate. It was a reminder of the gulf that now existed between Dempster and the heir to Swinging London, Cool Britannia.

Dempster had little access to the emergent upper class – the people of the new Lord Rothermere's generation – and even if he had been interested in them, they were not particularly interested in him. He tried of course, keeping abreast of the tangled romances of Jade Jagger, Piers

Jackson and Dan Macmillan. But one could tell in his writing that he didn't know them like his old chums. Nor was he at ease with the new cult – or type – of fame. One almost felt nostalgic to read in the diary that Baroness Izzy van Randwyck was leaving cabaret to take up acting. One felt a little bemused to learn from the same source that the 'Gladiator, Vogue, wants to be a TV presenter and pop star'. He never really did get so-called 'celebrity culture'.

But if it sat oddly on the page when Dempster reported that Kate Moss was currently dating 'Antony Langdon, 29-year-old singer with the group Spacehog', that might have been preferable to quoting his old drinking buddies. The antics of Dempster and his gang were becoming a bit hit-and-miss. When he dashed out of his office to tell roadmen to stop working because they were disturbing his train of thought, it was hilarious. But when he greeted a gay protest that was taking place on the balcony of the *Mail*'s atrium by shouting 'Jump! Jump!' – before trying to eject one of the intruders by force – he might have done better to keep a low profile.

On form, Dempster could still be the toast of the *Mail*. One afternoon, as was his habit, he was watching the racing on the office television when Michael Winner appeared on the screen, wearing a coat with a number of pockets and being interviewed. Dempster began ringing his mobile number, and every time the garrulous film director looked like finding his phone – which had 'Copacabana' as its ring tone – Dempster would hang up. He had his colleagues in stitches. But heaven protect you if you incurred his wrath. The staff in the newspaper's library might be bawled out for losing cuttings that he had forgotten to return. The technical support staff were subjected to daily tongue-lashings for his failings.

As for his pals, when he repeated Rupert Deen's observation in his column that 'pheasants were born to be shot, labradors to retrieve them, and Welshmen to go down mines', who was laughing? And Sir Dai Llewellyn's reaction to the news that arsonists had torched four of his six Welsh terraced cottages, bought and refurbished for rent, just seemed sad. 'I'll have a bottle of champagne and a claret, followed by a sea of vodka,' he said. 'Then it will all seem better.'

In the era of the TV confessional, to celebrate such a vice was in current parlance *inappropriate* – and it reflected badly on Dempster. When he arrived in the office sporting a painful bruise on his face, the assumption was that he had drunk himself under the table. At the *Express*, Hickey's John McEntee wondered if 'the victim of a scoop had resorted to fisticuffs?' Dempster's truthful reply – 'I hit my head on the door at home' – cut no ice. Even he assumed he had puzzlingly lost his balance. Today, it can be seen as another early symptom of his condition. And perhaps one can excuse his behaviour after his mother's death in 2000 on the same grounds.

It was not so much Dempster's unpleasantness to his sisters over his larger share of Topsy's inheritance that irked them. ('Where there's a will, there's a dispute,' says Erika.) It was more his seeming insouciance. They, after

210

all, had cared for her and sat at her deathbed while he had declined to visit. And though he joined them for Topsy's cremation at Golders Green – where a couple of songs by Hutch were played – he showed no enthusiasm about disposing of her ashes.

Born in Cornwall, Topsy retained a great love for the county all her life, regularly going to stay in Falmouth at the Greenbank Hotel. So happy was she there that she directed in her will that her ashes should be scattered on the River Fal – but neither sister felt inclined to put herself out further. Though Erika and her second husband had been in the habit of holidaying in Cornwall, staying on the Helford River, they were no longer doing so – and Pam had no intention of going down there. So they decided to deliver Topsy's ashes to their brother in a *fait accompli*: the onus would be on him to do the job. Together, they drove to Kensington, where Pam entered the *Mail*'s lobby and requested that the bag containing the urn should be put in his hands.

'And indeed it was,' says Erika. 'I believe his secretary was a bit twitchy having to look at it on her office shelf, but eventually the day came when Nigel wrote in his column that he had been to Cornwall to scatter his mother's ashes on the "River Helford". The wrong river! But never mind. She loved the Helford too.'

Perhaps more important than Topsy, Princess Margaret – once the best card in his pack – was dying before his eyes. In 1998, she cut short a visit to Mustique after suffering a stroke. Back on the island the following February, she had a bizarre accident in her bathroom. Attempting to rinse her hair in the shower, she appears to have fumbled the antiquated controls and directed jets of boiling water onto her feet. After a worried maid reported steam coming out from under the locked door, her private detective forced entry and discovered the princess in shock, her feet severely scalded.

Although Margaret shoulhave had treatment immediately, she delayed for some weeks, until it became clear that bad circulation – the legacy of years of chain-smoking – was preventing her recovery. Back in London, she refused skin grafts, with the result that she never regained full mobility. And after Dempster reported in June her first public engagement since the accident – for the wedding of Prince Edward and Sophie Rhys-Jones – there was little more good news. In August, his readers learned she was distressed that her son was to sell Les Jolies Eaux – recently gifted to him – and the following February that she was making her final visit to her old home in Mustique.

Rumours began to spread that Margaret had lost the will to live. And while her spirits revived after consultations at the Priory and – courtesy of Prince Charles – with an Indian holistic healer, the effects were temporary. She was soon felled by two more strokes, rendering her paralysed down her left side and blind in one eye, and was last seen in public on the Queen Mother's 101st birthday in August 2001. Wheelchair bound, with her arm in a sling, the invalid's face was twisted and her eyes hidden by thick sunglasses. Thereafter, she took to her bed, and died in her sleep six months later.

Writing a tribute in the *Mail*, Dempster called himself a 'court jester' to the princess – and provided a curious codicil to their relationship. In 1973, he had been driving her in a Mini Moke from Les Jolies Eaux to a 'jump up' on the beach at Mustique when 'my hand slipped from the gear stick and landed in one of hers folded on her lap, which immediately tightened around mine. As we arrived… she said to me good-humouredly: "Remember who I am and where you are." Only then did she release my hand.'

If this had some news value, the activities of another of Dempster's septuagenarian heroines had almost none, and his reporting of them seemed to be aimed at embarrassing a Greek billionaire rather than engaging his readers. John Latsis had been buying up Mayfair properties for a dec-ade – with the intention of developing a luxury apartment and office complex – and when necessary, re-housing pro-tected tenants further up Park Lane. However, the widow of a Lloyds underwriter, Mrs Gladys 'Bobbie' Stone was unwilling to relinquish the views of Hyde Park that she had enjoyed since the Sixties and in 1999 had to be evicted by court order. For the next year, Dempster relayed de-tails of Mrs Stone's travails (mainly focusing on the state of the carpets in her alternative accommodation) which culminated in a bathetic one-woman protest, when she stood outside her old dwelling with a home-made banner reading: 'Greek Revival Not Greek Tragedy in Mayfair'.

Meanwhile, Dempster's own tragedy was unfolding

between Kensington and Ham. As the world greeted the new millennium, the best his column could offer was a resolution list from the same old faces. Under the lead story – one Arabella Zamoyska hoped not to trip over her train while marrying the ageing actor Oliver Tobias – Sheridan Morley, Michael Winner, Frederick Forsyth and Ronnie Corbett added their own aspirations. And three days after finishing his teetotal January, not far from his weekend home, he was finally and fatefully caught drink-driving.

According to Dempster, he had been watching the English rugby team thrash Wales on television. According to his wife, he had been at the races. Whichever, he had drunk at least one bottle of wine before he hit a lamppost on a central reservation that intersected a zebra crossing. His Honda then spun across the road and bounced off several bollards before overturning. And on freeing himself from the wreckage, Dempster made straight for a branch of Wine Rack. Perhaps he intended to seek help, or to evade the law by purchasing and consuming some alcohol before the police arrived. Perhaps, in shock, he had gone onto autopilot and was pursuing his original mission to buy more booze.

Whatever his intention, it was no proof against PC Russell Yardley, who apprehended the culprit in the off-license. As the officer said in his statement: 'I saw a white man in a grey suit standing at the counter. I said: "Have you had anything alcoholic to drink?" He said: "No, nothing." His speech was incoherent and his eyes were glazed. I could smell liquor on his breath despite being a distance of at least three feet away.' While his car was transported to a garage, Dempster was taken to hospital for treatment to minor cuts on his hands, then driven to Richmond police station, where an intoximeter test showed the alcohol level in his blood to be almost twice the legal limit at 65 micrograms per unit.

FALL
'I Feel Very Discombobulated'

As ever, Dempster thought he could bend the law. He retained a solicitor called Robin Falvey, who specialised in challenging breathalyser tests, and had his day in court deferred until February 2003, when he appeared with six other defendants in a class action. This time, however, his luck ran out. At his sentencing in June, the judge called him a liar whose conduct was 'beyond contempt', banned him from driving for two years, fined him £1500 and ordered him to pay £840 towards the estimated £27,000 cost of the trial. But these were the least of his punishments: by then, the crash had cost him his marriage.

Camilla – who was now spending most of her time

in Ham – remembers that the day after his accident, her husband rang from the office and asked her to enquire of the garage about repairs to the Honda. 'Repairs?' she laughs. 'It was a complete write-off. They must have thought I was mad.' To her, it was further proof that Dempster's drinking was out of control. She had tired of his routine – 'coming home, downing three large vodka and oranges before dinner, then turning threatening and abusive'. Her self-confidence had been eroded by his constant attacks. Yet she knew she'd had enough. In August, when Dempster suggested they celebrate her 51st birthday, she 'couldn't go along with the hypocrisy any more' and told him she wanted a divorce.

It was agreed that she would keep the contents of both houses, and that he would receive half the proceeds from the sale of their house in Neville Terrace. But there was, she says, so much bad feeling that there was no verbal communication until it became clear he was mortally ill.

Had it not been for his drinking, that might have become obvious much sooner. There were signs, of course. Tessa Dahl remembers thinking 'he wasn't quite right' when she telephoned Dempster 'and he kept pausing, then repeating himself – he was pretending that he was trying to make himself clear, but you could tell he was covering something up'. Michael Corry-Reid noticed that 'Nigel was beginning to tell the same stories twice in a lunchtime, without noticing. And his driving was becoming frightening – he kept scraping the kerb'. His Friday cronies had other concerns, too. 'The deal,' says Michael

Corry-Reid, 'was that everything was off-the-record, but once or twice Nigel betrayed a confidence in his column.' However, rather than remonstrate, 'We decided to zip it when he was around, because we could tell he was ill.'

Emma de Bendern's daughter Atalanta, who was staying with Dempster in Neville Terrace, remembers that 'the only things in the fridge were caviar, grapefruit and bottles of champagne'. She frequently received calls from her ex-stepfather saying he had forgotten his keys and was locked out (and when he mislaid his car keys, he accused his wife of stealing them). He appeared, says Atalanta, to be 'in denial' – and making matters worse by his kneejerk mendacity. After the *Mail* top brass held a party at Mark's Club to celebrate a veteran sportswriter's 40 years in service, Dempster took a tumble on the steps outside, sustaining a twisted ankle, a black eye and a dent to his forehead. Although both his editor and proprietor had witnessed the incident – and were reportedly 'aghast' – the diarist claimed he had injured himself playing squash.

Moreover, Dempster seemed to have lost his judgement as much as his balance. His response to the destruction of New York's Twin Towers was to run two items of startling insensitivity. Four days after the biggest terrorist outrage in history, he divulged that one Bob Miller, founder of the Duty Free Shoppers Group, was worried his daughter had bought a house in uptown Manhattan; and three days later that the model Naomi Campbell had escaped death by missing her plane from Newark to San Francisco, on the doomed United Airlines Flight 93.

The modern world no longer agreed with Dempster. One of his assistants, Ulla Kloster, would urge him to 'revamp' the column, and Dempster's new battle cry became 'young, young, young'. But he showed no obvious enthusiasm for the cause. He was happier reporting that Lord Snowdon was giving up his house near Staplefield, or that Peter Cadbury's golf-cart had been hit by a van in the Bahamas. And while Paul Dacre realised that his once-great diarist still had a loyal following, he also knew that a new generation of readers expected the sort of C-list scurrility favoured by the *Sun*'s Bizarre page and its peppy rival in the *Mirror*, the 3am Girls. To that end, he poached John McEntee from the *Express* and put him in charge of 'Wicked Whispers', a column whose title and coy style were borrowed from the *Mirror*. 'Which multimillionaire gay rock star is sporting a new £500,000 diamond ring that says "F*** off" in precious stones?' asked McEntee. Even in his hamstrung state, Dempster could have guessed that one.

Now exiled to the back half of the paper, the diarist had his own way of dealing with old queens. There was something quaintly nostalgic about his tribute to the Queen Mother, who died at the age of 101 on 31 March 2002. The next day, Dempster's page was dominated by a cartoon depicting a race course finishing-line, seen from a deserted grandstand box. On the table rested a pair of binoculars, a granny's hat, a half-finished drink and a cup engraved 'Popularity Stakes: The Queen Mother, 1900-2002'. Captioned 'Clear Winner', around it were arrayed a selection of stories from the archive. Naturally, some old mates featured – among them Charles Benson, crawling out of the QM's box after a port-drinking session that left her unaffected.

He had one scoop left in him – the impending divorce of Bryan and Lucy Ferry – but this was small beer when the pressing matter of the day was Jade Goody's grope with PJ on *Big Brother 3*. Like the people he wrote about, Dempster was becoming an irrelevance – and an embarrassment, too. John McEntee remembers a lunch when Dempster turned on him, insisting he had killed his Peke Tulip. 'I said: "No, no, Nigel, I teased you about it [in print]." But he kept accusing me.' In the office, he had become a presence rather than a force, eventually only turning up for ten minutes a day. His staff compiled his page. A pretty assistant of Irish extraction called Bridget Christie* handled his paperwork – and Dempster asked this former acting student turned part-time stand-up comedienne to take him to his local Catholic church, the Brompton Oratory.

The management, concerned by Dempster's deterioration, convinced him to go into rehab at the paper's expense. 'But the first night at Farm Place, he climbed over the wall, and came back to Foxtrot Oscar,' says the

---

* It is said that Dempster had a 'massive crush' on Christie, who was 'loaned' to him by his employers for some months after his retirement. Returning to the paper, she used her experiences as the basis for a one-woman show, 'My *Daily Mail* Hell', which premiered at the Edinburgh Fringe in 2009 and has since toured. Married in 2006 to the comedian Stewart Lee, she is now part of the comedy aristocracy.

restaurant's then-owner Michael Proudlock. So there was something akin to relief at the *Mail*, when it became apparent that alcohol was only one source of Dempster's troubles. After he collapsed twice while playing golf with other executives in Le Touquet, he began to consult doctors and consultants about his condition – which due to its comparative rarity took over a year to diagnose.

Proudlock remembers him coming to Foxtrot Oscar 'covered in bruises'. Michael Corry-Reid recalls one occasion at Dan's, 'when, before he'd even had a drink, he keeled over into the flower bed – we thought he was dead.' And, continues Proudlock, 'The funny thing is, he didn't need to give up the Chablis. It would have made no difference in the end.' To Dempster's credit, however, he did. Admitted to the Cromwell Hospital for treatment on his elbow after a particularly nasty fall, he volunteered to detox on Antabuse – which combines with alcohol to make the patient violently ill – and stuck to orange juice for the last five years of his life. When Proudlock and Atalanta arrived at Neville Terrace to take him in, 'He looked so sad,' she says, 'like a little lost schoolboy.' And while Camilla had mixed feelings – 'I wasn't overjoyed that he'd do it for himself but not for me' – she came to soften after his death: 'Among his belongings, we found an old letter from me – I'd written it one "dry January", telling him how much more I appreciated him when he wasn't drinking – and that he kept it meant a lot to me.'

For now, all their exchanges were by letter, and it was in Dempster's handwriting – which shrank from neat to tiny – that the first clue to his condition was found. Another was his sensory confusion. (Atalanta remembers him complaining about an 'awful smell' that turned out to be heating soup.) And there were other indicators, too, including insomnia, terrible headaches and an aversion to light. Atalanta would return home to find Dempster sitting in the dark, unable to converse coherently. 'It was tragic,' she says. 'He could get choky on his food. His stare became fixed, because he couldn't move his eyes or turn his head properly, which made him even more scared of falling over.'

'In the beginning,' she continues, 'whenever I was concerned, he just said: "Don't worry about it." But eventually he became depressed, and had to take medication for that, too.' Cruelly, depression is a symptom of PSP – as well as an understandable reaction – but it did not entirely defeat Dempster. One night, Atalanta sat up at his bedside, 'and he was like his old self – his memory was back – and he chatted for about half an hour about his mother and father.' More likely, he would be at best wry. 'He stopped pretending everything was okay,' says Louisa Dempster. When Taki came to visit, her father told him: 'Inside this head, Mister Taki, there is nothing left.' And even the tough guy admits: 'I got a little teary.'

Dempster and his wife were granted a 'quickie' divorce in October 2002. But had he seen a subsequent item about the sale of Neville Terrace – in of all places the *Evening Standard*'s property-page gossip column – would he have laughed or cried? That the piece revealed Dempster was 'asking £1.75 million through former beauty queen and property agent Aldine Honey, whose Seventies romance with the reclusive property developer Harry Hyams the columnist once exposed' only proved his point about the spread of gossip to 'page 100'. That its author pointedly described the house as 'unmodernised' might have been taken as a dig at his own diary. But the fact that the writer of the story was the humbled Richard 'Daisy' Compton Miller — as a William Hickey, once the butt of Dempster'sjokes—mighthaveaffordedDempstersomeofthe *schadenfreude* others were enjoying at his expense.

Progressive supranuclear palsy is a terrible affliction. (The comic actor Dudley Moore had it, and like Dempster was commonly thought to be drunk.) At rapidly accelerating speed, sufferers can lose the power to see, speak, move, swallow or even smile. Rage, forgetfulness and depression corrode their minds while frequent falls batter their bodies. When their stares become fixed, they feel they are leaning too far forward and in correcting that perception tumble on their backs. In the end they die, not from PSP but from a weakened system. 'And the worst thing is,' says Proudlock, 'Nigel knew exactly what would happen to him.'

By and large, though, the news was remarkably slow to spread through his profession. In June 2003, when he arrived for the first day of his unsuccessful drink-driving trial, his gait was shambling and his appearance crumpled — a windcheater having replaced his old velvet-collared topcoat — but they were no deterrent to the photographer from the *Mirror*, sent to humiliate the great humiliator. Once, Dempster might have essayed a quip or even a pithy insult. Now, shielding his face with a newspaper and shouting, 'This is private, this is private,' he lunged at his tormentor, trying to grab his camera. 'He nearly walked into a tree,' said the snapper, who went on to report that at lunchtime, Dempster had run round the court house, again hiding his face and calling to his solicitor: 'Robin, they are trying to take my photograph.'

***

Dempster's name was trademarked, partly so that the *Mail*'s editor could use it to 'brand' a gossip page if he chose, and partly to prevent others from pinching it for the same purpose (as Dacre had done with 'Ephraim Hardcastle'). It was also agreed that his final diary should appear on the last day of his thirtieth year in charge. So, on 7 October 2003, he opened page 39 with a story about an adversary who he had been baiting for three decades – the Aga Khan – casting mild aspersions on the commitment of the 'blonde, pouting-lipped' German wife who was 20 years his junior. Around this dim innuendo were ranged three bits of harmless chit-chat, about American *Vogue*'s Plum Sykes, the smart writer Julian Fellowes and Earl Spencer (formerly Viscount Althorp). Below was a mischievous piece speculating that Tony Blair might elevate Peter Mandelson to the peerage and give him the old Lord Chancellor's lavish apartments. And in the basement, there was a rather touching – and telling – PS:

> 'Well-fed cook Clarissa Dickson Wright begs me not to reveal that she is about to become a bankrupt. However, when she learned that today's diary is my swansong, Clarissa quickly changed her mind. "Go ahead then – it will be an honour to be in the last Dempster column."'

That someone – even a good sport – should be 'honoured' to have her shame paraded across a paper would have been inconceivable 30 years before. It could only happen now because Dempster had become a sort of national treasure. How different from his first column as diary editor, when he exposed Lady Annabel's pregnancy by James Goldsmith and began a 20-year feud. But in many ways, how little had changed. The rest of that page had been of no greater interest – and probably less – than its ultimate successor.

Along with two anodyne pieces of European royalty, on 8 October 1973 Dempster's other offerings included: an item on traffic wardens' attempts to explain their work to 'rotary clubs, women's institutes and church-based groups'; paragraphs revealing that George Melly was in line for a film role, the Duke of Beaufort had bought a new hunter and an MP had nearly had a car accident; and an estimate of the money raised in synagogues to support the Yom Kippur war.

So why was Dempster considered so dated by the end? Of course his novelty had worn off over 30 years.

More importantly, he had not adapted fast enough to the 'dumbing down' of society and the media. The genteel doings of a well-spoken elite could not compete in the mass-mind with the outrages perpetrated by Premiership footballers. As Dempster took his leave, two players from Leeds United were being questioned over an alleged rape. A week earlier, four more had been accused of raping and 'roasting' a teenager.

Dempster received a different type of roasting from his erstwhile rivals. Reflecting on his retirement, the *Telegraph* called him 'out of date' and 'out of touch'. The *Guardian* quoted the writer Henry Porter: 'Even in his heyday, you didn't know who the hell he was talking about most of the time. They were all slightly louche and connected with horse racing or Annabel's.' The *Independent* claimed his column was concerned with 'the comings and goings of a largely irrelevant group of people'. And a week after Dempster's last bow, in a *Times* piece headlined ,'Another day, another so-called competitor falls by the wayside', Andrew Pierce of the 'People' page revealed that Richard Kay had refused to take over the *Mail* diary if it was to be 'branded' as Dempster's – and cheekily stole the name for his own column that day.

The *Mail* gave their veteran a mixed send-off. At Bridget Christie's suggestion, his staff gave him a Bible, to acknowledge his increasing interest in Catholicism. Dacre held a gathering of half a dozen executives – but Dempster only stayed a couple of minutes. The management arranged that his pension should be paid as a lump sum split into five yearly instalments ('so he couldn't spend it all at once,' says Camilla). Geoffrey Levy, his friend since the Sixties, wrote an affectionate tribute, which dwelt on his generosity – when a librarian lost most of his savings, 'Nigel's was the biggest cheque to go into the pot to help the man get back on his feet' – and ended with a typically boastful quote: 'No one could have invented a better gossip columnist than me.'

However, the public arena, where the young Dempster had thrust himself uninvited, now became a frightening place to him. He talked to Ed Victor about writing his autobiography, and Victor tried to ease his evident money worries by encouraging him ('although I knew nothing would come of it'). More often, he would say to his daughter Louisa, 'I just want to go home', meaning the house in Ham. After PSP was diagnosed, Camilla agreed to take him back when his situation became untenable. And while she still doesn't regret the divorce, she told him that she would never have pressed for it had she known he was ill.

Nicholas Haslam once encountered Dempster in the street, confused and in his dressing gown. Mostly, though, he tended to lurk inside – listening to the radio when he could no longer focus on the television, placing rash bets with his bookie by phone – unless Michael Proudlock could cajole him out to lunch at Foxtrot Oscar. For several years, the stocky, rubicund Proudlock would drive round to Dempster's home and transport him to his old haunt. When his friend found walking too difficult, Proudlock would physically carry him into the joint.

'At first it was every day,' he says, 'and we would always drop in on Charles Benson at his hospice in Battersea.' (Dempster's old tipster was to die of cancer in 2002.) But it grew harder and harder to coax him out. 'He became unsure whether he wanted to see anyone – or rather, for them to see him – and I found that if I told him people were coming to meet him at Foxtrot, he wouldn't go out.'

In the end, Proudlock worked out a strategy. He always put Dempster at a table in the far corner of the restaurant. Then, if friends or colleagues hoped to catch him, they were seated at the next table. It could be a distressing experience: Dempster tended to dribble masticated food down his chin. But Adam Helliker and the travel writer Victoria Mather were among the many who came to pay their respects.

Mather had adored Dempster since her first visit to El Vino's in the late Eighties, when he knocked down a lout who attacked her for wearing trousers – and she was not alone in her affection. After the divorce and house sale, Dempster was never short of female company at the under-furnished ground-floor flat he now rented in Onslow Gardens. He had Christie and a Filipina nurse called Alice Young to help at first – and later, two or three nurses to provide round-the-clock care. He became very close to the portrait painter Fanny Rush. Camilla and Louisa covered for Alice on her days off. His sisters made contact again – as did Tessa Dahl in a visit which she and Richard Kay both agree was memorable. 'He asked me to marry him,' says Dahl, 'and I don't think he was joking.' 'She told

Nigel she'd had a boob job,' says Kay, 'and he asked for a feel.' On both occasions, if not with equal sincerity, she said yes and Dempster followed up on of his proposals.

No saint, then, but Dempster still had his sights set on heaven – or a miracle. Quite why this lifelong atheist became a Roman Catholic is a matter of some dispute. Several of those close to him claim that Christie 'converted' him, while she has said that 'he was going towards it anyway'. Since his detox, he had regularly attended meetings of Alcoholics Anonymous – above all a 'spiritual' programme that requires belief in 'God as we understand him'. Perhaps Dempster's admiration for Christie convinced him to adopt her beliefs.

Regardless of the reason, he was confirmed at Brompton Oratory in 2004 – but what did he expect from his newfound faith? According to his family, 'he was hoping he'd be cured' and 'he was superstitious, not religious'. The next year, accompanied by Christie and her sister, he joined a pilgrimage to the French shrine of Lourdes, in a last-ditch attempt to save his body if not his soul.

By then his finances were ailing, too. Dempster's outgoings – his rent, his nurses' wages, his betting and horses' livery fees – far exceeded the settlement made by the *Mail*, and he was burning through his savings. While he could still write, he sent letters to many of his wealthier friends – 'He sounded down on his luck,' says Anna Wintour – and Taki for one reacted magnanimously, contributing £25,000 towards his care. But Dempster was not beyond philanthropic gestures himself. When the

October Club charity chose the PSP Association as the beneficiary of its annual dinner in 2004, he agreed to feature in a ten-minute film about the effects of the disease.

It was heart-wrenching – ironically, the most effective and affecting broadcast he ever made. Rod Gilchrist, by then deputy editor at the *Mail on Sunday*, had worked with Dempster over the years – supplying interviews to ITV in which the diarist met such minor royalty as Princess Michael and Princess Stephanie of Monaco – and had always found him oddly awkward in front of the camera. The print journalist can be unctuous to an interviewee's face, but later venomous on the page. To achieve the same effect on the small screen – undermining one's subjects while appearing to admire them – is a special skill that Dempster did not possess, so it was as if he was fighting with one hand behind his back.

Now, intercut with clips of him chuckling on chat-show sofas with Terry Wogan and Derek Jamieson, he was shown in his shabby flat, sitting on a park bench and kneeling in church. His features were frozen, his frame shrunken in his once-tight suit, his tie adrift. There was stubble on his face, and the remains of his hair stuck up from his scalp. In an expressionless voice, he expressed so much misery: 'On a bad day, I stay in bed, because I feel very discombobulated… My voice is very querulous and um, um, I get forgetful – forgetful – I suppose.' Christie joined in: 'There are not many things he enjoys, except the Oratory. It gives him focus and – 'purpose,' interrupted Dempster – 'purpose'. 'I miss my freedom and my friends,'

231

continued Dempster. 'They don't come round at all. And I miss being able to laugh.'

'I don't know why he said that about his friends,' remarks Proudlock. 'It must have been a low point.' But if he was unfair to many of his circle – who put themselves out much more than Dempster ever did for his dying parents – this was still a bravura performance. The effort to find words like 'discombobulated' and 'querulous' must have been immense. Within six months, it seemed beyond him.

In controlled circumstances, he could still perform (and dissemble). When Ross Benson died from a sudden heart attack, he gave a quote to the *Evening Standard*'s Londoner's Diary: 'We were true enemies when he was William Hickey, but when he came to the *Daily Mail* I gave him a lunch of caviar and lobster. I will be missing a day at the Cheltenham Festival to attend his funeral.' But at the wake, John McEntee remembers Dempster, haggard, dishevelled and shrouded in his windcheater – approaching him simply to bark his surname. 'He didn't have any conversation. He couldn't. It was as much as he could do to put a name to a face.' Dispiriting though it must have been for the Shirburnian who knew every boy in his school, it was somehow in character.

***

At the end of 2005, Dempster was in distinguished company – chosen as one of 40 journalists to have their photographs hung in a permanent collection at the National Portrait Gallery. Celebrating 40 years of the *Press Gazette* trade paper, selected by the most influential editors of recent times, the *Press Gazette* Hall of Fame honoured 'the men and women who have shaped the modern era of British journalism'. That it included such literary giants as Bernard Levin and Cyril Connolly indicates the esteem in which Dempster – the boy who threw his books from the verandah – was held by his own profession. But one couldn't help noticing that half its icons were either retired or dead.

Dempster's active life was all but over. He could still walk – indeed his constant pacing was a cause of concern to his carers – and he could still talk, though indistinctly. But his discombobulation was now so advanced that, had he not gone back to Ham in February 2006, he would have been placed in a hospice. He was lodged in a down-stairs annexe, and had two nurses by day. Eventually he became bedridden, and his communication dwindled from thumbs-up and -down to a gurgle, then a flicker of the eyelids. That this energetic, quick-witted, curious man – he of the prodigious memory, a more entrancing speaker than he ever was a writer – should have come to this was a genuine irony. Almost karmic, said his victims, but hardly any thought deserved.

He paid rent at Ham, which made it easier for his ex-wife. Camilla says Louisa was insistent on this arrange-ment (and his daughter, along with Carolyne Waters had power of attorney). While he could still talk, the local priest came round to hear his confession – and later to give absolution – but that didn't stop him contemplating assisted suicide. His sister Pam recalls watching a television documentary on the subject with him, when he said, 'I left it to late.' Camilla discussed it with him, too, 'but it wouldn't have been fair on Louisa.' So the emphasis was on cheering him up.

Most of Dempster's good friends – including a loyal posse from the *Mail* – would troop out to Ham and talk across his bed about the old days, or feed him spoonfuls of scandal. Jack Martin – his long-time Hollywood informant and a man who would not have been out of place in a Frank Capra movie – would drop by for a day at a time and pepper him with yarns. McKay and Kay were frequent visitors. (When Tina Brown heard that they had been reading him her new biography of Princess Diana, she broke down in tears.) And Adam Helliker remembers Dempster waving his hand across the Common, which he took as a reference to his 'neighbour' Lady Annabel Goldsmith.

A gossip to the end, Dempster died in the early hours of 12 July 2007 'from a general weakness of the system', says Camilla. And while he had no obituary in *Heat* magazine (where a week later Jade Goody was voted the 25th most important person in the world) the traditional press could not afford to ignore him. Under the cloak of anonymity, most were not very kind. But in the *Independent*, where such pieces are signed, Michael Leapman said he 'set the pace and standard' for gossip writing – adding that, although his branch of journalism was not regarded as heroic, 'Dempster's strength was that he approached it with great seriousness and took pride in doing it better than anyone else.'

There could be worse epitaphs. There could be better funerals. Dempster's was held at the Brompton Oratory six days after his death, and attended by 40 or so mourners: friends, family and colleagues (not to mention Dempster's vet and his wife). It was a solemn affair, with music by Fauré and Bach, and a reading from the Book of Widsom that seemed apposite to the diarist's later years: 'If they experienced punishment... their hope was rich with immortality. Slight was their affliction; great will their blessings be.'

However, the ceremony struck some jarring notes. The gospel described the Sermon on the Mount, when Jesus promised blessings to the type of person that Dempster seldom was. The gentle and poor in spirit? The righteous, merciful and pure in heart? The peacemaker? Many of the congregation must have struggled to reconcile their memories of the departed with the ideal candidate for heaven. Nor were matters helped by the priest's timing in the homily. 'He was a bit too slow,' recalls Richard Kay. 'He said, "Nigel may spend a million years in purgatory" – and paused just long enough to shock everyone – before adding that in eternity it would pass in the snap of a finger.' It's the kind of story Dempster would have embellished in a bar, or told more mundanely in his column – the kind that was swapped with relish at his St Brides' memorial service in October.

Four months seems to have wrought a change in Dempster's popularity. ('I think there was a certain amount of guilt from people who'd written him off,' says Michael Cole.) Hundreds converged on the church, threatening to spill onto Fleet Street. Charles Collingwood and Louisa gave the readings, while Charlie Brooks and Paul Dacre delivered the addresses. Dempster's old editor said Dempster was credited 'for better or worse' with creating 'the celebrity gossip industry', continuing: 'I would humbly suggest, however, that Nigel, with his panache and his wit, was on a different planet from the so-called 3am Girls.'

The congregation was played out to the strains of *Well, Did You Evah? What a Swell Party This Is* – and perhaps Dempster was lucky to have left it early. The press was not as it had been. After the funeral, when Jack Martin dropped into the *Mail* to make some telephone calls, he was asked to keep his voice down – in a newspaper, for goodness sake. Meanwhile, Dempster had enabled such a transformation in the media and society that he no longer had a place in either.

On the day of writing, the biggest gossip story in Britain – and it's even bigger on the net than in print – concerns the wedding of the surgically enhanced and addicted soft-porn model Jordan to the martial artist and *Big Brother* winner Alex Reid. (Jordan arrived at church swearing, after avoiding photographers and film crews who had not paid for access.) What authority could the old diarist bring to that? 'And he would have hated Ascot these days,' says Nicholas Haslam. 'All those trashy people. Nigel was the standard-bearer for Society. He wanted to keep that flag flying.' Even Dempster's local lunch spot, where once he could consort with the remnants of his formerly fast set, is unrecognisable today. Foxtrot Oscar is now part of the culinary empire owned by Gordon Ramsay, a failed footballer turned chef, whose precarious pile has come from franchising a name partly made through swearing at wannabes on television.

Of course there is a twist. Dempster hankered after the very fame and fortune that television confers. But as the public seemingly preferred the notion of him to the reality, he may as well have been a fictional character. So considering the amount of odium he endured for what he represented – much more than for what he published – he almost earned a fair wage.

After 25 years of reckless spending, and four of ruinous care bills, his material legacy to Louisa was little – a couple of hundred thousand pounds from which, to the amazement of his family, some £20,000 was deducted for bequests to three Catholic priests. He left his brain to science, and one hopes it can reveal as much about his social pathology as his PSP. As for his legacy to humanity, look around you.

This very afternoon the publisher of *OK!* magazine has bought the television station Channel 5. Richard Desmond, who made much of his fortune from such publications as *Asian Babes* and *Penthouse*, plans to air exclusive footage of celebrity weddings. In the Westminster village, it is reported that a Twitter group – hiding behind a remote server in California – pools tittle-tattle from the corridors of power. In the digital age, gossip envelopes us. People make fortunes creating it about themselves. They taint impressionable minds with shamelessness and false expectations. The young equate it with fame.

Who's to blame? Society? The media? They reflected and changed Dempster, and he them. They still reflect and change each other. Both have been democratised and cheapened in the last 50 years – while deference now seems to be bought not earned.

Perhap it was ever thus? Then should one long for the old hypocrisy, which the aphorist called 'the tribute vice pays to virtue'? Surely not, when that means our 'betters' – if such a concept still exists – can behave outside the (increasingly lax) bounds of acceptable behaviour. Almost no one could regret that our cheating parliamentarians were exposed for over-charging their expenses. And it was the gossip – the moat cleaning, the duck house – that brought the story alive.

This is a complicated issue – and as Tessa Dahl says, Dempster was a complicated man. Only his particular circumstances could have created him, but only he could have made his particular life from those circumstances. He presented a world that was as much a product of his imagination as a reflection of reality, and the same is true of the way he presented himself to the world. He was both snob and iconoclast, breaker and keeper of confidences, outsider and insider. A moralist and a hedonist, he was loved and hated in equal measure – and sometimes by the very same people. A bully with a thin skin, he defined an age and was defined by it. He was an important yet ephemeral figure. And he was fun. To Camilla, her ex-husband prompts parallels with his fictional hero, Jay Gatsby. 'And like him,' she says, 'nothing about Nigel was really what it seemed.'

PS Word reaches me of an unquiet grave. Three years after his death from progressive supranuclear palsy, a disease akin to Parkinson's, Nigel Dempster's family still has to decide where to scatter his ashes, which for now are resting in the hall of his second wife's £2 million house overlooking Ham Common. As you read here first, the socially ambitious scribbler, who died at the age of 65, left the bulk of his six-figure estate to his daughter Louisa, and she has the final say on the resting place of his charred remains. Comments her mother Camilla: 'There has been talk of Richmond Park or a racecourse. He used to go running in one and loved the other.' The track or the turf? Watch this space.

INDEX

Aga Khan 225
Aitken, Jonathan 88, 199
Al-Fayed, Dodi 194, 197,
    200–202
Al-Fayed, Mohammed 170, 190, 193,
    194, 198–202
Althorp, Viscount 181–183, 201
Andrew, Prince 142, 151
Anson Lady Elizabeth 65
    Party Planners 51
Antabuse 222
Argyll, Margaret Duchess of 91
Aspinall, John 92, 93
Attalah, Naim 161

Bankhead, Tallulah 27
Barry, Stephen 131
Barton, Tony 119
Basualdo, Luis 167–169, 175, 176,
    186
Beaverbrook, Lord 45
Beckwith, Tamara 194
Behind Palace Doors 178
Benson, Charles 85, 117, 136, 137,
    169, 221, 229
Benson, Ross 103, 112, 154, 197,
    198, 232
Berens, Jessica 175, 176
Berens, Richard 137
Bernard, Jeffrey 74
Bird, Mynah 195
Birley, Mark 84, 93
Birley (Goldsmith), Lady Annabel
    84, 234
Blair, Tony 225
Blandford, Marquess of 187
Blood injury syndrome 205, 206
Bogard, Gary 109

Bond, Alan 185
Booker, Christopher 74
Booth, Pat 67
Bordes, Pamella 160, 161
Bosley, Deborah 161
Bowerbank, Christopher 35
Bowles, Peter 156
Boxer, Mark 179
Bradshaw, Jon 46, 60, 62, 65, 76,
    163, 173
Branson, Richard 180
Brewer, Liz 55, 91, 109
Bristol, Marquess of 171
Brocket, Lord 194
Brooks, Charlie 136–139
Brown, Craig 207, 208
Brown, Tina 109, 110, 114, 143,
    175, 176, 179, 234
    Life as a Party 113
Buccleuch, Duke of 134
Burton, Richard 84

Cadbury, Peter 99, 132, 160, 220
Caine, Michael 173
Callaghan, James 90
Callan, Paul 82, 83
Cameron, David 194
Campbell, Naomi 219
Carrington, Lord 131
Chan, Jacqui 119
Charles, Prince 116, 131, 132, 154,
    160, 196, 197
    marriage problems 141–143
Christie, Bridget 221, 230, 231
Christie, Carolyne 58, 131, 170
Clarke, Ossie 67
Cole, Michael 135, 193, 20, 236
Colin, Pamela 119

Collingwood, Charles 36, 37
Collins, Joan 170, 173
Colquhoun, Maureen 91, 92
Compton Miller, Richard 224
Connolly, Richard 146, 147
Constantine, King 15, 16, 88
Cook, Peter 157
Corbett, Ronnie 62
Corry-Reid, Michael 114, 218, 222
Cowell, Simon 86
Cox, Jeremy 36
Creer, Erica 102

Dacre, Paul 184–186, 189, 198,
  206, 220
Dahl, Tessa 100–104, 107, 109,
  115, 142, 218, 229, 238
Daily Express
  decline 81
William Hickey column. see
William Hickey column
Daily Mail
  branded gossip page 225
  class system, and 113
  compact, becoming 82
  Craig Brown working for 208
  diary 82
  Fleet Street, leaving 174
  importance of Dempster to 116
  Paul Tanfield column 35, 40, 41
  power, becoming 81
  Quentin Crewe column 41
  re-launched 71
  revival of 82
de Bendern, Atalanta 219, 222, 223
de Bendern, Emma 67–70
de Savary, Peter 149
Deen, Rupert 60
Dempster, Angela 'Topsy' (née
Stephens)

ashes, scattering 211
background 24, 25
death of 210, 211
Hampstead, flat in 38
Hutch, affair with 27, 28
infidelities 26, 27
Jersey, not settling in 37, 38
morals 26
Nigel, doting on 26, 38, 39
pastimes 25, 26
Dempster, Eric Richard Pratt (Demy)
battles with Nigel 26
death of 153
family 24
India, working in 24, 28, 29
Jersey, settling in 37, 38
nature 25
pioneer family, from 24
Topsy's morals, attitude to 26, 27
Topsy, adoring 25
Dempster, Erika 26, 28, 30, 31,
  36, 38, 43, 53, 98, 158, 210,
  211
Dempster, James Pratt 24
Dempster, Jock 24
Dempster, Lady Camilla (née
Osborne 70, 96–100, 103, 204,
  217, 218, 233, 239
divorce 218, 223
relationship with Nigel 107, 108
Dempster, Louisa 70, 99, 205, 233,
  237, 239
Dempster, Nigel
aggression 204, 209, 210
anecdotes, hijacking 72
ashes, unscattered 239
assistants, treatment of 16, 17
attacks on 110, 111
attitude at school 36
battles with Eric 26

betting 136
birth 26, 29
blood injury syndrome 205, 206
bookmaker's bills 44
Britain, return to from India 31
businesses at school 35
campness 15
Catholic, becoming 230
childhood 29–31
Common Entrance, failing 33
crammer, attending 39
Dacre, relationship with 184–186, 189
Daily Mail, at 71, 72, 82–89
de-tox 222
death of 234
deb circuit, on 39–43, 49–51, 54, 55
decline 185–187, 193–215
decline in value 14
Diana, taking to 199, 200
divorce from Camilla 218, 223
documentary about PSP 231
drink driving charges 115, 116, 175, 205, 214, 215, 217, 218, 224, 225
drinking 94–96, 218
drugs, taking 153
early jobs 44, 45
Eighties, in 149
environment, as creature of 176
family antecedents 23
family holidays 33
fight at Epsom 108
finances 169, 170, 230, 231
first marriage 67–70
foreigner, as 23
friendship, flair for 32
funeral 235, 236
gatecrashing 49

Goldsmith, feud with 84, 85, 188, 189
Good Morning America,
appearances on 141
guest, as 65, 66
hell-raiser, as 55
Helliker leaving 203, 204
himself, gossiping about 115
Hislop, mutual loathing 145
home, lack of 33
horses 16, 135–139
illness 222
illness becoming apparent 218, 219
impatience 189
inability to read at schools 32
India, born in 23
infidelities 100–104
informants, paying, 169, 170
judgement, loss of 219
last column 225, 226
last years 228–234
legacy to Louisa 237, 239
Lloyd's, at 40, 41, 49
London Marathon, running 115, 130, 131
looks 34
losing touch 208, 209
louche life 42
lunches 94–96
Mail on Sunday column 148, 149
Manhattan, in 56, 57
marriages, announcing 90
name, change of 158
nursing 229
office, as seen in 91
office, no longer force in 221
parents, attitude to 38
part, playing 113
pension 227, 228

popularity 16
power, love of 78
pranks on 207–209
Private Eye, return to 157
private party, at 114
Queen, at 62
rehab, in 221
relationship with Camilla 107, 108
resignation from *Daily Mail* 146–148
rivals, roasting from 227
school, at 31–37
second marriage 70, 96–99, 103
send-off 227
sensory confusion 223
Sherborne, at 34–37
softer, becoming 177
sphere of work 14
tax-efficient company, earnings channelled through 169
television documentary 90, 91
temper 16
trademarked name 225
TV chat show 115
upper classes, chronicles of 13
vanished world of 18
well-off women, penchant for 58
Who's Who, entry in 158–160
writing style 85, 86
Dempster, Pam 26, 38, 39, 70, 71, 211, 234
Dempster's People 206
Desmond, Richard 237
Devonshire, Duchess of 133, 134
Diana, Princess 116, 152, 155, 170, 187, 194, 197, 234
affair with Dodi 199–202
bulimia 143

Charles, making unhappy 142
death of, 202
Dickson Wright, Clarissa 226
Digital age, gossip in 237, 238
Discos 55, 56
Dolin, Si Anton 134
Douglas-Home, Robin 119
Drug taking 153
Dugdale, Rose 43
Dunnett, Carmel 47
Dupree, Michael 57

Earls-Davis, Major Michael 35
Edge, Carol 102
Edward, Prince 152, 212
El Vino's 73
Elwes, Dominic 92, 93
Emin, Tracey 149
English, David 82, 111, 144, 147, 148, 162, 184, 206
Esser, Robin 54
Establishment, collapse of standards 14
Evans, Peter 166, 178

Faber, Anne 54
Fellowes, Julian 54, 55, 146
Ferguson, Major Ron 151
Ferguson, Sarah 87, 151, 152, 178
Ferry, Bryan 187
Ferry, Lucy 187
Fisher, Francesca 171
Fleet Street 73, 74
newspapers leaving 174
Foot, Paul 74
Forte, Lord 146
Fraser, Lady Antonia 87–89
Fraser, Sir Hugh 87, 89
Freud, Lucien 188

Gibbs, Bill 67
Gilchrist, Rod 83, 91, 111, 112, 231
Gilliatt, Penelope 40
Goldsmith, James 84, 85, 92–94, 110, 288, 289
Goldsmith, Jemima 189
Goldsmith (Birley), Lady Annabel 84, 234
Good Morning America 141
Goody, Jade 221, 234
Gosling, Sir Donald 204
Gossip columns in New York 56
Greig, Geordie 15

Haden-Guest, Anthony 46, 55, 60, 61, 71, 76, 159, 188
Hall, Jerry 149
Hamilton, Neil 199
Harmsworth, Vere 77, 78, 81, 82, 85, 110–112, 206
Harris, Robert 98
Harry's Bar 16
Hart, Derek 119
Haslam, Nicholas 56, 114, 121, 126, 132, 148, 228, 236
Heath, Ian 57
Heiress: The Story of Christina Onassis 169
Helliker, Adam 18, 148, 202–204, 229, 234
Hello! 179, 180
Hervey, Lady Victoria 194
Hewitt, James 185, 187
Hislop, Ian 145, 146, 156, 157, 162
Hoare, Audrey 58, 59
Hobbs, John 69, 70
Honey, Aldine 224
Hunt, James 132

Hussein, King 15
Hutchinson, Leslie 'Hutch' 27–29
Huth, Angela 119
Hyams, Harry 224

Ingrams, Mary 161
Ingrams, Richard 74, 145, 145, 156–158, 160–162

Jagger, Bianca 132
Jagger, Mick 132, 149
James, Clive 87

Jamieson, Derek 231
Kay, Richard 112, 185, 187, 200, 234, 235, 227, 229
Kennedy, Tessa 93
Kerman, Nicky 94, 134
Khashoggi, Adnan 185
Kidd, Johnny 99
Kimberley, Earl of 45–48, 53
Kitt, Eartha 47
Kloster, Ulla 220

Lambton, Lord 88, 133, 134
Lamont, Norman 146, 147
Langan, Peter 172–174
Langan, Susan 173
Lasson, Sally Ann 181–183
Latsis, John 213
Lawman, Clare 168
Leeds, Duke of 96, 97
Legh, Diana 47
Lever, Harold 64
Levy, Geoffrey 63, 71, 228
Lichfield, Patrick 46, 50, 54, 61, 62, 65, 76, 86, 119, 185, 206
Life Unfulfilled, A 117, 129, 130
Lindsay-Hogg, Lucy 119
Litchfield, David 159

Llewellyn, Dai 72, 114, 121, 122, 169, 188, 210
Llewellyn, Roddy 117, 119–129, 145
Lockwood, Victoria 181
Logue, Christopher 74
Loss, Joe 49
Lownes, Victor 114
Lucan, Lord 92
Lycett Green, Rupert 88
Lytton's Diary 156

Mackenzie, Colin 58, 63, 64, 135, 136
Maguire, Mickey 47
Mail on Sunday 148, 149, 179
Mandelson, Peter 225
Marentette, Danny 176
Margaret, Princess 27, 43, 47, 64, 66, 71, 108, 173
  A Life Unfulfilled 117, 129, 130
  dalliances 119
  death of 211–213
  marriage 117–121
  Roddy Llewellyn, relationship
with 120–129
Marina, Princess 27
Marsden, Simon 68
Martin, Jack 234, 236
Mather, Victoria 229
Maudling, Caroline 54
Maxwell, Robert 147
McEntee, John 197, 205, 210, 220, 221, 232
McKay, Peter 57, 58, 71, 76, 77, 100, 136, 157, 161, 187, 198, 234
McNally, Paddy 151
Media, history of 13
Merchant, Vivien 87, 89

Michael, Prince 64
Michael, Princess 149–151
Middle-aged women, downfall of 195
Miller, Bob 219
Miller, Jonathan 62
Mills, John 56
Minelli, Liza 131
Mirren, Helen 127
Monckton, Rosa 200
Moore, Dudley 173, 224
Moorsom, Christopher 98
Morgan, Piers 86
Morton, Andrew 142, 143, 185, 186
Moss, Kate 209
Mountbatten, Edwina 27
Moynihan, Colin 160
Murdoch, Rupert 81

National Portrait Gallery 233
Neil, Andrew 160, 177
Nigel Dempster's Address Book 178, 186
Norris, Steve 187
Novello, Ivor 27

O'Mard, Kevin 171
Oberon, Merle 27
Onassis, Aristotle 165–167
Onassis, Christina 132, 165–169, 175
Osborne, John
  The World of Paul Slickey 40
Osborne, Lady Camilla. See
Dempster, Lady Camilla (nee
Osborne

Packer, Kerry 185
Palmer-Tompkinson, Tara 194

Palumbo, James 208
Parker-Bowles, Andrew 185, 187
Parker-Bowles, Camilla 116, 144,
   185, 187
Parkinson, Cecil 144–146
Patton, Charlotte 24
Patton, Louisa 24
Pearson, Lucy 132, 167, 168
Pearson, Michael 62
Pekinese dogs 176, 205, 221
Philip, Prince 147
Pierce, Andrew 227
Piggott-Brown, Sir William 45, 62,
   102, 114, 195
Pinter, Harold 85, 87, 78
Pitman, David 63z
Plumtre, George 201
Polizzi, Lady Olga 146
Ponsonby, Lady Sarah 126
Porter, Cole 27
Porter, Henry 227
Press
   celebrity circus, transformation
into 13
   public's interest, about 14
Private Eye 67, 71, 74–76, 92–94,
   156–162
   Grovel column 74–77, 112, 130,
145, 146
Progressive supranuclear palsy 224,
237
Proudlock, Michael 221, 222, 224,
   228, 229, 232
Punch 190, 194

Queen magazine 40, 41, 44, 62
Queen Mother, death of 220

Racehorses 16, 135–139
Radcliffe, David 32

Ramsay, Gordon 237
Rendall, John 126
Rhys-Jones, Christopher 31
Rhys-Jones, Sophie 31, 212
Rhys-Jones, Theophilius 31, 33
Ritz magazine 159
Roberts, Glenys 57, 63
Robertson, Neil 40
Rogers, Byron 79
Rothschild, Jacob 88
Royal Dempster's 186
Royal reporters 143
Rufus-Isaacs, Lady Jacqueline 66,
   119
Rufus-Isaacs, Lord Antony 43, 48,
50, 60, 61, 65–67
Rush, Fanny 229
Rushton, Willie 74

St Germans, Elizabeth Countess of
   195, 196
Sangster, Robert 149, 185
Self-promotion 181, 182
Sellers, Peter 119
Services rendered, tips for 169
Seward, Ingrid 102
Sheffield, Samantha 194
Shilling, Mrs 134
Shorto, Roberto 171
Simons, Maggie 48
Simunek, Nick 65
Sissons, Kate 189
Slater, Colin 57
Smith, Dr Patrick 125
Snowden, Earl of 66, 75, 117–121,
   220, 207
Soames, Emma 179
Somerset, Lord David 88
Soskin, Tania 128, 129
Spencer, Countess 114

Stephens, Jack 24, 31
Stephens, Robert 88
Stevens, Jocelyn 129, 130
Stone, Gladys 213
Stringfellow, Peter 128
Sun 81
Swallow, Timothy 143

Tatler 109, 179
Tennant, Charlie 171
Tennant, Christopher 171, 172
Tennant, Colin 118–121, 124,
    171, 172
Tennant, Henry 171
Thatcher, Denis 90
Theodoracapulos, Taki 72, 78,
    100, 138, 188, 223
Tholstrup, Mogens 194
Tory, Peter 134
Townsend, Peter 118
Trelford, Donald 160
Tremlett, Diana 34
Tryon, Lady 'Kanga' 144, 195–197
Twin Towers, destruction of 219

Van-Hay, Geoffrey 73
Victor, Ed 112, 134, 178, 228
von Bulow, Claus 131

Walsh, Brian 68
Waters, Carolyne 233
Waters, Roger 131, 170
Waugh, Auberon 74, 75, 88, 89,
    156, 157, 189
White, Marco Pierre 178
Whitehouse, Mary 62
Wiggins, William 170
William Hickey column 45, 53, 57,
    63–66, 73
  death of 154

resurrection of 197
Wilson, Christopher 108, 137, 142,
    154,
Wilson, Harold 64, 90
  resignation 118
Windsor, Lord Frederick 149
Winner, Michael 177, 209
Wintour, Anna 46, 59, 60, 103, 153,
    154, 175
Wintour, Charles 59
Wogan, Terry 135, 231
Wood, Garth 60, 109
Wright, George 153
Wyatt, Steve 178
Wyndham, Violet 121

York, Duchess of see
Ferguson, Sarah
'You Can Judge a Man By the
Company He Keeps' 62
Young, Alice 229

A freelance writer and editor, Tim Willis has worked for most of Britain's national newspapers and some of its glossier magazines. He is also the author of *Madcap* (Short Books, 2002), a well-received biography of Pink Floyd's 'crazy diamond' Syd Barrett.

In case of difficulty in purchasing any Short Books
title through normal channels, please contact
BOOKPOST Tel: 01624 836000
Fax: 01624 837033
email: bookshop@enterprise.net
www.bookpost.co.uk
Please quote ref. 'Short Books'